My Enlightening Heart Disease

Dr. Abhay Bang

Translated from Marathi by
Dr. Arun Jatkar

Popular Prakashan
www.popularprakashan.com

Published by
Asmita Mohite for
POPULAR PRAKASHAN PVT. LTD.
301, Mahalaxmi Chambers
22, Bhulabhai Desai Road
Mumbai - 400 026
info@popularprakashan.com

First published in Marathi as *Maza Sakshatkari Hridayrog* by
Rajhans Prakashan Pvt. Ltd., Pune, in January 2000

Address: SEARCH, Shodhgram, Chatgaon, Dhanora Taluka,
Gadchiroli - 442605. Email: search.gad@gmail.com
First Published in English by Popular Prakashan Pvt. Ltd.: 2025

(4612)
ISBN: 978-81-982623-0-1

Front cover design: Satish Deshpande, courtesy of Rajhans Prakashan Pvt. Ltd.
Layout design & Illustrations: Courtesy of Rajhans Prakashan Pvt. Ltd.
Typesetting: Anjali Sawant

PRINTED IN INDIA
by Printone Graphics
A - 309, Byculla Service Industries
Byculla (East), Mumbai - 400027

Twenty years have come and gone
and I am still at the dance,
I guess that God just changed his mind
and gave me another chance.

And on that day I took a vow
to let go of the past,
to live my life and love each day
as if it were my last.

— Jill Warren
(A cancer survivor)

The information in this book is based upon my medical knowledge and understanding developed by testing some of it in my own life. However, human body, manifestations of disease and response to therapy all may vary from person to person. Hence, those with heart disease are advised to decide level of exercise and choice of medicines in consultation with their physician. Medical science is constantly changing, evolving. The medical information in this book is as of the year 1999.

— Dr. Abhay Bang

Preface

(To the original Marathi edition)

Three years ago I suffered a sudden heart attack. Did my heart disease really arise all of a sudden? Or was it happening each day for several years; only that I became aware of it one day and thought that it happened suddenly? How did I feel when I became a patient? What cause did I discover for my heart disease? What did I do to recover from it? And how, instead of my heart disease being treated by me, did my heart disease treat and work on me? How did the close encounter with death affect me? And how am I living the renewed lease of life today?

This entire episode was personal. But not sharing it with my friends would amount to deliberately keeping them in dark about the risk of heart disease. An intense desire to alert them compelled me to write about it in the form of a long letter to a few select friends. Without my knowledge, a friend sent it to the leading Marathi daily *Maharashtra Times* which published that letter. Mr. Sada Dumbre, editor of the well-known Marathi weekly *Saptahik Sakal,* suggested that I should write a much more detailed account of my heart disease. That long article, titled *Maza Sakshatkari Hridayrog* (literally, 'My Enlightening Heart Disease'), was published in the Diwali special issue of *Saptahik Sakal* in 1996.

Carl Rogers, the well-known psychologist, used to say, "Things we consider most personal are the most general!" There was something in my personal story of heart disease that touched the heart of the people. As if everybody was suffering from the same pain and each one was searching for some solution. The response to that article was unprecedented, as if the entire Maharashtra identified itself with it. This book is a far more detailed version of that article. The search that began with coming to know about my heart disease took me far beyond the realm of mere physical illness. Later on, that search of the 'beyond' became the focus of my attention. The journey continued even after I wrote the article for *Saptahik Sakal*. I have included the details of that journey in this book. In addition, the final chapter of this book contains information that may be useful to the patients of heart disease and to people who are sincerely interested in not becoming the patient.

Writing this book has been a very joyful experience. My role is that of a narrator. This is a travelogue describing the event of my heart disease and my journey into the depth of my own 'being'. To present a purely scientific description or a comprehensive philosophical position is not the intent of this book. Nor is this book a scientific discourse on medicine, yoga or spirituality. What I experienced is the theme of this narrative. I have tried to tell my story as honestly as I could. Naturally, this story relates to my life and tells about the outer and inner places I visited during my journey. It does not mean that I intend to deny the existence of other paths and other places; it is just that I do not know about them, I did not visit those places. I do not claim that the path I followed is the only right way. There is nothing 'right' or 'wrong' in this story; it is simply a narration of what took place.

And this story is not over yet. Something new happens each day. This is my story as of the 4th of September, 1998. Tomorrow, on the 5th of September, something new could happen. How could I possibly guess that today?

I must mention one thing. More than a thousand readers wrote to me after they read my letter in the *Maharashtra Times* and the article in *Saptahik Sakal*. Though I wanted to, I was not able to reply to these letters. I could not respond to this avalanche of personal letters while carrying on my medical work among the tribals in the Gadchiroli district. I regret the fact that while I thoroughly enjoyed the warmth and affection expressed in these letters; I could not reciprocate on an individual basis. Each letter was dripping with emotions! What could I possibly write back to them? And how? It was as if Lord Krishna had come to the tiny, modest hut of Vidura! I do not know how to be a good host to Him! It seems I will always remain indebted to these readers.

I see a long line of people, who already are suffering or are likely to suffer from a disease like mine. I have attempted to narrate the story of my heart disease in the hope that it will ease their journey to some extent. If that really happens, I wish to dedicate this service to life itself which blessed me with heart disease and then brought me out of it by holding my hand.

Shrikrishnarpanmastu.

(May this be my humble tribute to Lord)

— ***Dr. Abhay Bang***
4th September, 1998
Shodhgram, District: Gadchiroli
Maharashtra - 442605, India

Publisher's Note

Dr Abhay Bang is a well-known physician, trained at Johns Hopkins in the US. As one brought up at the Sewagram under Gandhi's 'Nai Taalim' he started 'Shodhgram', a township near Gadchiroli with a hospital and a research centre, deep within India, in a predominantly Adivasi region and devoted himself to providing medical facilities, health awareness, and de-addiction from alcoholism to the local people. Since he had medical knowledge, simple regular habits and blessings of the people around him, suddenly facing cardiac problems thirty years ago was a shock to him as well as to others.

His Marathi narration *Maza Sakshatkari Hirdayarog* was a book based on his study as a medical researcher with himself as his patient. Even as he was being admitted in a Nagpur hospital he carried with him standard works on cardiology. This unique study by a doctor who is his own patient makes fascinating reading, particularly as Dr. Bang recovered and is continuing his important work at Shodhgram.

As the problem of heart disease and lifestyle has become even more urgent and pressing, it was necessary that this Marathi writing that has gone into twenty-five editions is also available to English language readers, and maybe through English, to other language readers as well.

Fortunately, Dr Arun Jatkar, an admirer of Dr. Bang made available an English translation and we, at Popular Prakashan, have great pleasure in presenting it to wider audiences.

— ***Ramdas Bhatkal***
Publisher
Popular Prakashan

Acknowledgements

Many individuals have made important contributions to the making and shaping of this book.

During and after my illness, my wife Rani remained steadfast by my side and looked after me. She lovingly bore the burden of my explorations and journey without complaining. Sometimes she made useful suggestions, but never insisted; never interfered with whatever I did. She is the closest witness to my journey; she is also my most intimate audience.

I wish to remain forever in debt of my teacher and cardiologist Dr. P.S. Bidwai, my spiritual guide Vimalatai Thakar and finally of Vinoba Bhave, who met me several times during this journey by way of his books and helped me fathom the deeper meaning of spirituality and Sanskrit texts.

I learnt from the writings of Dean Ornish and several individuals and organisations involved in the field of health and yoga. The letter titled as 'The happenings within me' that I wrote to my select friends on the completion of one year after my heart attack might have remained a personal and private account, revealed only to that close circle, and may never have led to this book. However, Mr. Pralhad Jadhav arranged to get that letter published in the Maharashtra Times and then Mr. Sada Dumbre saw to it that I wrote a detailed article for the Saptahik Sakal. Mr. Dilip Majgaokar of Rajhans Prakashan reached out to me several times while I was working in the forest of Gadchiroli and insisted that I ought to write this book and undertook the responsibility of publishing it in Marathi.

What followed was like a fairy tale. People of Maharashtra widely received the book with open arms. The Marathi book is currently in its 25th edition.

Dr. Arun Jatkar, a Marathi scientist working in the USA for nearly thirty years, took upon himself the responsibility of translating the Marathi book into English. His selfless inspiration and the commitment to perfection revealed so often during the process of translation amazed me. I just cannot thank him enough. It is due to his untiring efforts that this English version has become possible.

Shri Ramdas Bhatkal took upon himself the arduous task of correcting the English translation, and finally, getting the book published by the prestigious Popular Prakashan. I am grateful to him.

Thousands of readers and patients urged me through direct contact as well as by way of letters. The oft-revised manuscript was carefully typed on computer by Mr. Balvant Surve. The scientists, sages, saints and intellectuals in whose thoughts and experiences I sought strength and support at every step are my predecessors. I continue to seek guidance from them as I follow the path.

Without all these people, this book would not have been possible!

— ***Dr. Abhay Bang***
Shodhgram
January 2025

Contents

1. Thunderbolt

Life is what happens to you when you are busy making other plans.

— John Lennon

1.1

On the morning of April 18, 1995, I left home for morning walk. We have named our settlement in the forest as 'Shodhagram' - The Search Village. That is where we have established our hospital for tribals, our research and training centre for village health and the de-addiction centre. That is where we live in the Gadchiroli district in Maharashtra, India. The district is remote and very poor. An average man in Maharashtra either has not heard of Gadchiroli, or heard of it for its forests, tribals, snakes, malaria and Naxalites, an ultra-leftist movement.

I walked up to the entrance gate of Shodhagram. Our two Alsatian dogs, Shera and Soni, ran ahead of me while our two Pomeranian dogs, Mita and Rupi, sauntered right behind. Shodhagram is surrounded by deep greenery. This is '*Dandak Aranya*', the very forest described in the great Sanskrit epic *Ramayana.* A narrow, winding path of red earth runs across the forest from Shodhagram to the nearby village Kudakvahi. This is the path I take every morning.

After walking a short distance I felt a sudden sensation of pain in the chest, as though someone had gripped me in a very tight embrace. The pain soon spread to the left arm. In the past, I had felt similar pain on a few occasions, and after all medical tests, it had been diagnosed as heartburn caused by acidity. I sensed that the pain today was rather severe as though the heart muscle itself was hurting. I wondered if it was 'angina'. I returned home and chewed several antacid tablets. If this pain were merely heartburn, I thought, the antacid tablets would neutralise the acid in my stomach and the pain would go away.

I left for the walk again a little later. Now Rani, my wife, also accompanied me. I had barely walked a hundred steps before the pain returned. "Should I tell Rani? Oh, no! She will get extremely worried." I forced myself to walk a little more. But the pain soon made it impossible for me to walk any further. "Rani, I cannot walk anymore! I am in pain!" Something snapped in my mind right there and then. This was not just acidity. This was a "heart attack"!

Deep inside I knew it was a heart attack. But the intellect demanded scientific, medical evidence. With slow and deliberate steps we made it back. I was immediately hooked up to the ECG (electrocardiogram) machine. The nurse tore off the recorded strip and handed it to me. Both Rani and our nurse Nanda looked on with curiosity and anxiety. With wires still taped to my chest, I examined my own ECG. Rani is a gynaecologist. We did not have any other physician on our staff besides me. Nagpur, the nearest city, was 200 km away. I was forced to interpret my own ECG. Today it was not normal. The S-T segment of the ECG had slipped down the 'normal' position. So my chest pain was not innocuous after all! I told this to Rani, and within two minutes she announced – "We are leaving for Nagpur! Right now!"

With a great flurry of activity the preparations began. Anand, our elder son, was in the ninth grade and had gone to the Gadchiroli town, 16 km away, for his annual examinations. We could not meet and tell him anything before we left for Nagpur. We managed to convince the nine-year old Amrit, our younger son, that we would be back the same evening or latest by the next morning. I asked Rani to pack a couple of books on heart diseases. "What do you need those books for? There are well-qualified doctors to treat you there!" she said. "Yes, but I need to understand what has gone wrong with me," I replied.

I slipped a tablet of Sorbitrate under my tongue. It helps increase the blood supply to the heart. I explained to Rani what to do should my heart suddenly stop or should I suffer an intense pain in the chest and collapse on the way to Nagpur. She packed a few emergency medicines and we left for Nagpur.

The car raced towards Nagpur. I kept poring through a book on ECGs. What was the meaning of the change I saw in my ECG today? I suddenly remembered that twenty years ago, when I was preparing for my degree of M.D. in internal medicine, we, the young resident doctors, were possessed by ECGs and the texts on ECGs. To detect the subtlest changes in ECGs, to interpret them and to diagnose the associated heart maladies had become our most passionate pastime. We would toss the ECGs at each other and challenge to diagnose the problems from these. It was a very thrilling pastime. But I had lost my touch with ECG in the last fifteen years. Shodhagram is situated in the middle of tribal[1] settlements and one rarely comes across a heart disease patient, leave aside a patient who has suffered a heart attack. So it had been ages since I had looked up a text on ECGs.

The Sanskrit epic *Mahabharata* tells a story of Arjuna, the greatest archer. When Arjuna and his brothers and cousins were being trained in archery, their Guru tested their abilities. Arjuna alone could aim an arrow at the eye of a bird sitting on a tree. While taking the aim, every other prince continued to see the sky, the tree, and its branches, Arjuna saw nothing but the bird's eye. Today, while poring over books I had become like Arjuna. I could see nothing other than the minor change in the S-T segment that I had noticed in my own ECG. My mind was busy trying to interpret that change. "What will be my diagnosis?"

The car was racing towards Nagpur. Deep inside me there was turmoil. "What has happened to me? Is it going to be something sinister? Deadly...?"

We reached Nagpur by afternoon. Immediately, we went to Dr. P.S. Bidwai, the senior cardiologist. Twenty years ago, when I was his student and junior colleague, he had taught me about heart diseases, but also loved me like his son. Today, on seeing me in his cabin, he thought I had come to pay him a courtesy visit. He was delighted to see his favourite student, and started discussing about

---

1. *The tribals of Gadchiroli district belong to the aborigine tribe called 'Gond'.*

a new intriguing patient of his. I interrupted him and said, “Sir, I have come today as a patient. I had pain in my chest this morning!”

He looked at me with a surprise. I was merely 44 years old. His mind was not prepared to accept that Abhay could have developed heart disease. He took my medical history, examined me thoroughly and took my ECG once again. His face grew serious. My chest pain was diagnosed as “Unstable angina or Non-Q Wave Infarction”[2].

“You must get admitted to the hospital immediately”, he said. There was no longer any doubt. It was real, it was serious. I had to be admitted to the hospital immediately.

As I was leaving Dr. Bidwai’s office, I noticed two thick, red-cover books on his desk. These were two volumes of the world renowned book ‘*Heart Disease*’ written by Eugene Braunwald, the Professor of Medicine at the Harvard Medical School. I had wanted to read this book for a long time, but never had the opportunity. Today, many questions were raging in my head. “May I borrow these two volumes?” - I asked Dr. Bidwai. For a moment he seemed to ponder over the wisdom of letting an emergency patient read about his own disease. But he was a teacher to the core. How could he ever tell his student not to read those two volumes? “Take them along”, he said. Rani carried those two hefty volumes for me. By four in the afternoon, I was lying in a hospital bed. I had become a heart disease patient. Me, a heart patient!

Both Rani and I were shocked. One recurring thought possessed me. “I might suffer a massive heart attack right here in the hospital and die in the next 48 hours; may be next week. What then? What will happen to Rani? What will happen to Anand and Amrit?

How could I possibly leave this world so soon? Without fulfilling my responsibility towards them? Our institute SEARCH which we had founded in Gadchiroli, its activities, its commitments? Our campaign against alcohol? What is going to happen to all of these? Do I have the right to die like this?”

---

2. *Unstable angina is the first episode or sudden increase in angina. Infraction is an area of tissue that is dying due to insufficient blood supply. Most heart attacks are diagnosed in the emergency room.*

The more I thought, the more I realised the gravity of the situation. Suddenly I sensed the real danger. "Hey, I have not 'lived' my life yet and the death has arrived? You mean, the END? What nonsense! My life has hardly begun. Yesterday, only yesterday, I was that little boy walking to the kindergarten. There! That is me with a schoolbag on the shoulder. And that little boy is going to die soon? Oh no! Not so soon, oh please! I have so much to do, so much to live. I have yet to understand the real purpose of life. And the end is already here!" With no warning whatsoever, the sand had shifted beneath my feet. The foundation beneath the edifice of my life was slipping. All my assumptions, everything I had taken for granted, all the calculations I had made...everything was falling apart.

I was not prepared to die. I had taken a very long life for granted and had been postponing, even avoiding, the real living. I was saying all along to myself, "Let me just do this, just this much today and from tomorrow I will start living a real life, I promise, from tomorrow, I will really begin my life!" So far I was only acting as if in a dress rehearsal. The real play was yet to begin…And here the curtain was about to fall!

1.2

Not just the fear of death, but many other questions harassed me. "How did this happen to me? What could I have done to deserve this punishment? And why did not I, a medical doctor, wake up any sooner?" But did it really happen all of a sudden? Did it pounce upon me without any prior warnings? I started remembering the past events, one by one...

Just the previous night, on 17th April, I was sleeping on our terrace as we often do in summer. Our younger son, Amrit, got out of his bed around two in the morning and came out to lie down beside me as he does quite frequently. He still needs the security of his parents' company at night. I cuddled him and softly patted him to sleep.

That is when I felt some pain in my chin. Who would bother about a mild pain in the chin at midnight? I ignored it and went back to sleep. The thought of what this pain might turn out to be the very next day did not occur in that half-awake state of mind. In fact, the pain of a heart attack can be experienced in the chin or lower jaw. But I did not suspect.

For the past few days I had noticed some pain in my chest while riding a bicycle or playing team sports. The pain used to be located in the middle of my chest and used to spread to my left arm. The pain was similar to what is called 'angina'. When the supply of blood to the heart is reduced due to narrowing of arteries from within, one suffers from angina. The angina is precipitated when the heart does not receive the increased blood supply it needs - for example during a period of hard physical labour or after dinner or when one is excited.

But there were some puzzling features which were against calling my pain 'angina' with certainty. Many times, even when I was engaged in an intense physical activity such as jogging or exercising with 'bull worker', I had experienced no such pain. A year ago, I had climbed 1500 steps to the top of Raigad fort and had felt no pain whatsoever. I had taken my ECG several times and nothing 'abnormal' had been detected. Yet the suspicion had lingered in my mind. So I had consulted a cardiologist friend of mine. He had twice submitted me to a 'stress test', in which my ECG was taken while I was made to exercise on a treadmill. The treadmill is a machine, which makes one walk on a moving belt. The belt speed can be varied from 'very slow' to 'very fast'. By tilting the moving platform upwards, more strenuous walking exercise such as climbing up the stairs or a hill can be simulated. The faster the belt is made to move, the faster you must walk, which begins to strain the heart. The heart rate soon begins to rise above the normal resting rate to fulfil the demand of increased supply of blood and the attendant supply of oxygen to your heart muscle. If the blood vessels are constricted, the blood supply to the heart will not keep pace with the demand and the ECG pattern will deviate from normal.

Both the times I took this test, my ECG had appeared normal. So, it was concluded, that my chest pain must be due to something else, most probably a sensation of heartburn caused by hyperacidity, and not angina. Now, while lying in the hospital bed, I began to regret that had we not made the error in diagnosis, my heart disease could have been detected a full year ago!

I remembered that more than a year earlier, my blood cholesterol level was found to be 244 mg. A level of 150 to 240 mg. is medically considered 'normal'. However, there are two kinds of cholesterol -- HDL (high-density lipids) and LDL (low-density lipids). HDL is 'good' cholesterol, while LDL is the 'bad' one. A high level of HDL helps keeping the heart healthy, while a high LDL predisposes heart trouble. My blood LDL level was higher than normal and the HDL level was lower, so it was wrong both ways. But I had somehow convinced myself that a total cholesterol level of 244 was only 4 mg more than 240, the upper limit of normal. All I needed to do, I thought, was to control my temptation to feast on milk cream. "If only I had been more careful since then, I would not be lying in this hospital bed right today!" Now I repented.

Nearly two years earlier, I had discovered that I suffered from diabetes. The diagnosis had come as a shock to me, the mind refusing to accept that I was a diabetic. Apart from the rising level of sugar in blood, diabetes also promotes the narrowing of most blood vessels. I had indeed begun to take medicines for my diabetes and that had brought my blood sugar under control. However, I had neglected to initiate the other precautions for preventing the narrowing of blood vessels causing heart disease. Why did not I take the precautions? Like a workaholic then, was I completely absorbed in the campaign against alcoholism. I was chasing the ideal of bringing about a social change. For that I had to work hard, keep on working harder. I was examining patients every day, prescribing to them the rules of healthy living. But I had no time to practise what I preached. What was the need? Me...developing the heart disease? Impossible!

And then, while lying in the hospital bed, I remembered what happened five years earlier. In 1990, I had spent three months in the USA for studies. I carried back huge trunks filled with books, notebooks and research publications. When I arrived at the airport in New York, my flight for India was waiting. There are no porters to cart away a passenger's luggage at airports in Western countries. So I loaded my heavy trunks on a trolley and started pushing it towards the check-in counter. At one point, I had to strain hard because of the upward slope. Suddenly there was pain in the chest. I barely managed to continue pushing the cart. Rested for a while. The pain abated considerably. However, I was anxious. That was the very first time I had experienced pain in my chest. "What could this chest pain be due to?" -- I wondered, "Certainly not a sign of heart disease! I was only 39. How could I even think of a heart disease at such a young age?" Besides, my US health insurance had lapsed just a day earlier. If I had sought medical aid for my chest pain, I would have been certainly hospitalised. Medical tests and treatment are so expensive in the USA that it would have financially ruined not just me, but my future seven generations! I had to make a very tough decision.

My flight was waiting at the departure gate. I boarded the plane and sat down in my seat. I reached India safely, without any medical crisis. A few days later I saw my cardiologist friend. He put me through the paces of the 'treadmill test' till I was perspiring. But the ECG remained 'normal'. We both agreed that the chest pain at New York airport was probably a muscle pain; nothing to worry about. Looking back, it seemed that it was the very first manifestation of my heart disease. "If I had not missed its significance and had begun a proper treatment then", I thought, "the state I was in today would not have arrived. I was stupid!"

Going further back, I remembered that ten years earlier, when I was 34 or 35, I had begun to sense that my body was no longer in the fittest condition; I no longer had the strength I once had; muscles had begun to lose their tone. It was just after Rani and I had both finished our post-graduate studies in public health in the Johns Hopkins University in the USA and returned to India. We were busy with preparations for the work we had planned to start in Gadchiroli. I had once thought that I should commence daily exercise and sports. But then, I was only 34. A 'mission of life' awaited us. I was ready to go at it with our full strength. Exercise could wait for the present. So also the sports. It was time to devote to my avowed mission. "There will be plenty of time to attend to exercise and sports later on", I had rationalised, and "I will certainly take up regular exercises someday. Not now, but later on". Thus the idea was postponed.

My mind wandered further back. Twenty-five years ago, when I was in a medical school in India, I had read in the books on pathology that narrowing of blood vessels (atherosclerosis) typically begins after the age of 50. However, post-mortem examinations conducted in the West on children who had died had shown that the process of atherosclerosis could begin even at such an early age. The implication was that the preventive measures to avoid heart diseases should begin in childhood. When I had first read about this twenty-five years ago, I had easily convinced myself that this was nothing more than an "American fad". It cannot happen in India. People in India live a 'natural' lifestyle, not an artificial and stressful lifestyle like they do in the USA. We do not need to worry about these heart diseases. Later, much later, when I will be past 50, I will need to be careful, but not now! Not when I was only 20!

Today, as I remembered all this, I felt remorse. Nature had tried to warn me again and again. But each time I had ignored the warnings. I had avoided doing anything and had chanted the mantra, "later!". What if I had not ignored those warnings? What if I had acted then? Indeed, if I had not acted then, death would not be knocking on my door now. Why did I not wake up earlier?

I did not wake up then and now I was lying in a hospital bed!

1.3

In twenty years since I started practising medicine I had diagnosed serious maladies in thousands of patients. I had witnessed hundreds of deaths. But now, for the first time in my life, I was a patient and I was gaining first-hand experience of the fear of death. I carry in mind a dim and foggy memory of how the first seventy hours passed in grim anticipation of an impending heart attack. Everything around me felt unreal. The lines of demarcation between truth and illusion had become faint. "Am I going to die?" I thought the first night in the hospital, "this could very well be my last sleep. If the heart attack strikes while I sleep, I may not see the next morning. What I see around me right now might be the last sight!" I kept talking to Rani till late in the night and after that I kept awake reading. Since there was every possibility that I might pass away sometime during the night, I wanted to 'live' as much as I could!

Some ten or twelve years back, while I was a student in the USA, I had seen a Gary Cooper movie '*High Noon*'. The story begins with the news of three dangerous criminals who escaped from a prison and plot to come back to take revenge against the sheriff who had caught them in the first place. The entire town becomes gripped with fear of these hardened criminals actually returning. The very thought strikes terror in everyone's heart. There is no actual violence depicted in the movie. But the dark shadow of a bloody fight holds one in a vice-like grip. That is how I felt about the impending death. "Will the death strike? How? When? And what will happen when the death does arrive? This game of life will be over forever."

The dull routine of life now suddenly became very beautiful and desirable. I still remember the very first breath I drew when I woke up the next morning in the hospital. It brought the awareness that I was still alive. I turned my neck and stretched my legs. "I can still use my muscles! What a grace! I can make movements with them! They are mine!" I looked downward. I could feel the muscles in my neck contract to let me turn the neck downward. "Oh! This life is so beautiful! I can turn my neck whichever way I want! Why did I not experience this joy earlier? Now, if I am given a second chance, I will feel the joy every time I turn my neck..."

During my stay in the hospital I craved to meet my sons. The day after I was admitted to the hospital I said to Rani, "Please call the children and have them come to see me." She wanted me to settle down in the hospital first. "If they come and see you like this, they will be shocked", she said, "and carry the permanent fear that their father has developed heart disease. Better wait till your condition stabilises." I am generally not very aggressive or stubborn (or so I believe!). But my desire to see my children was so strong at that time that I said to Rani, "I must meet my sons right now!" and I turned my face away from her.

Rani understood. She arranged for our sons to come to Nagpur from Gadchiroli. Little Amrit ran towards me calling out in his sweet voice, "Nayana!" Children call me 'Nayana'. Rani is from the southern state, Andhra Pradesh and her mother tongue is Telugu. In Telugu, "Nayana" means father. "Nayana", Amrit asked, "what happened to you? Did you get a heart attack?" Anand, our elder son, was trying to appear more mature. He tried to tactfully silence Amrit's innocent questioning. I held them both firmly in my embrace, very close to my chest. People often say in India that you cannot happily close your eyes forever without first seeing your children to your heart's content. There is also an idiom in Marathi like "the quest of my eyes was satisfied". Up until now, these expressions had been mere words to me. In order to understand them in real sense you must personally experience the full potency of these words. My life was an uncertainty. I wanted my children to be with me.

I suddenly remembered. When we decided to build a hospital in Shodhagram for the tribal people, they told us what bothered them most. "Doctor *saheb*", they said, "the government hospitals admit the patient, and throw out relatives. But we want to live amongst our relatives and die amongst our relatives". So, when we built the hospital for them, we built a series of little huts, where a patient could indeed live with his or her relatives. The tribal people were thrilled and overjoyed by this idea. Now I realised that not only the tribals, but I too longed for the company of my own flesh and blood when a life-threatening disease struck me. I could see the tribal people of Gadchiroli in my mind. I could almost hear the old tribal village leader Sambhaji Darro ask, "So you too are like us, eh Doctor *saheb*?" I answered, "Yes, Darro Patil[3], we are all alike!"

My mother accompanied by my brother and his wife came to see me. My father, who was travelling, soon followed them. My mother is 72. What must she have felt when she saw me, a 44 year old, lying in the hospital bed with a heart attack? I dared not see her eye-to-eye. I was sick and yet I felt guilty!

My wife Rani was a constant companion during my stay in the hospital. What would happen to me should I die was a lesser question than, "What will happen to her?" But she had no time to vent her own grief and anxieties. She shouldered the entire burden with confidence never revealing the immense mental agony she suffered, kept a smiling face and managed everything efficiently. We had been married for 18 years. I fell in love with her once again as I lay in the hospital bed. I did not want her to be away from me even for a moment. "Who knows, when death may pounce on me". Was I seeking support to hold onto in that threatening situation? I cannot tell. But one thing was certain. If death were to close in on me, I wanted Rani to be beside me.

1.4

But fear was not my main feeling. I felt sad, agonised at the thought of life slipping away from me. However outwardly, I was behaving as if nothing serious had happened to me, as if I was admitted to the hospital for cough and cold. I was talking to people, I was laughing and I was also reading a lot. They say that soldiers experience no pain at the moment of death because their minds are benumbed protecting

3. *Patil is a traditional title of a village chieftain.*

them from pain. While I was hovering on the border between life and death, I felt similarly.

The chest pain did not reappear. I was resting in bed and taking medicines. For three days in a row I felt no chest pain. Gradually, I began to entertain the probability of surviving. Not only that, but I even started wondering, "Did I really have a chest pain three days earlier or was it simply a figment of my imagination?" On the fourth day, I carried out a secret experiment on my own. To be honest, I am ashamed to tell anyone about this, but I must reveal everything. I had to know for sure that the chest pain I had felt was really angina and not a simple transient muscle pain. "Are we making unnecessary fuss over a minor illness? I must determine!" I thought. So, first I paced my own room back and forth several times. Nothing happened. I counted my pulse and I walked faster and faster. I was hoping that nothing would happen and I will throw away that label of heart disease. I increased the speed further. As soon as my heart rate sped up to 110, the chest pain returned. I immediately stopped my experiment and quietly lay down in bed. My heart disease was real! The diagnosis was correct! Looking back, I realise that my experiment was amazingly stupid. It makes me feel ashamed of myself. How risky it was! But it also makes me laugh at myself. I had hoped to discover that there was nothing seriously wrong with me. Oh, how powerful is one's wishful thinking!

My grief was twofold. Like any human being, I did not want to die. In addition, the fact that in spite of being a medical doctor I misdiagnosed myself was both insulting and embarrassing. Why did my diagnosis go wrong? My medical ego was shattered. I had not been just a 'good student', but had topped in the University in almost every examination in my medical career, both in India and abroad. My CV flaunted three gold medals, but that made the humiliation worse. What was the use of all those honours if I could not diagnose my own disease correctly? I was wrong all these years! And it was not just me. My friends who had specialised in cardiology had also been wrong. How could this have happened? This was the second reason for my grief.

Despite the fact that I was a medical doctor and despite my frequent suspicions, medical tests failed to confirm that my chest pain was due to angina. Why did our diagnoses go wrong? Ample exercise during the treadmill test had not produced the symptoms of angina or any changes in the ECG. This had misled us. As I read the bible on heart diseases by Dr. Braunwald, I found an eye-opening piece of information.

The sensitivity of the treadmill test is only 75%. That means, if a very large number of patients suffering from the real heart disease were given the treadmill test, this test will indicate the presence of a heart disease in only 75% of such patients. (In other words, the test will not detect the presence of a heart disease in 25% of patients, even if the patients did have the heart disease!) For a test to be fully sensitive, every patient who has a heart disease must test 'positive' for heart disease. A simple ECG at rest has sensitivity of 30% and the treadmill test has a sensitivity of 75% when used for testing angina patients. However, the medical textbooks which I owned did not mention this fact. Only Braunwald's textbook contained this valuable information. Moreover, a recently published study on this subject in the *New England Journal of Medicine* found the treadmill test to be no more than 55% sensitive! In the absence of this information, we had blindly believed in the results of treadmill tests! Even though the chest pains strongly suggested angina, we had relied on the negative results of the treadmill test and ignored the warning signals my heart was sending.

In medicine, a patient's own account of his ailment is called 'history'. This history is extremely important for making a proper diagnosis. However, with an ever-increasing reliance on the machines and medical tests, we, physicians, have begun to downplay the patients' own accounts, i.e. the medical histories. What happened to me was no different than what is happening to patients at large. We ignored my 'history' and unhesitatingly relied on the treadmill test.

I had a feeling of intense dissatisfaction and guilt that the diagnosis of my own heart disease had eluded me for a long time. Then the renowned medical journal '*Lancet*' brought out a special issue on heart disease. The guest editor of this issue was an internationally well-known expert on heart disease. He had written, "Last year when I suffered a heart attack, I delayed seeing a physician for 72 hours despite persistent chest pain. I felt very guilty about this stupidity of mine. So I asked ten internationally renowned heart specialists who had suffered a heart attack to recount their own experiences. All ten specialists had either misdiagnosed themselves, or had avoided any testing or had delayed seeking the treatment."

So I was in a good company of world-famous heart specialists! I felt less guilty. But I realised that we physicians often go wrong when it comes to diagnosing our own disease.

While lying in the hospital bed, I read Braunwald with insane avidity. In the first three days I had read nearly eight or nine hundred pages out of the most informative fifteen hundred pages of that book. Many of my wrong ideas were getting dispelled. The darkness was being replaced by illumination. That made me smile. Such is the joy and glory of gaining knowledge! And at the same time, the lurking hideous thought cropped up in my mind, "How long would I be able to experience this joy? Is my time to enjoy this over?"

A vicious wheel of questions turned round and round in my head. "What is my true diagnosis? What has happened to me? A downward slippage of the S-T line in the ECG by half a millimetre could very well be an instrumental error and may have nothing to do with my heart condition. How wonderful it would be if that indeed were the case!" The second question was more serious. "How much life do I have hereafter?" In a mad frenzy I turned the pages of Braunwald's book and searched the answers to my nagging questions. The book contained tables of the probability of survival -- a month, a year and five years after the onset of angina. It also gave information on the probability of fatality associated with various sets of symptoms and medical indicators. If this complication is present, the patient has so much probability of dying. I was trying to decipher my own prognosis from the vast array of information the book provided. I was searching for the verdict -- how much time was left at my disposal. "How long will I live"?

1.5

One more question bothered me -- "Why should this suffering be my lot? How on earth did this happen to me?" My parents, both in their 70s, were still healthy. My aunts and uncles were 70, 75 and 80 years old and hale and hearty. My grandmother, who passed away two years earlier, lived to a ripe old age of 107 years! And here I was only 44! I was not fat, I did not smoke, I did not live in urban area, I lived amongst the aborigines and I did social service work. So I was quite sure that I would not suffer the diseases of affluence -- obesity and heart disease. I had assumed immunity from these ailments. These diseases afflict others. Those who contract these diseases are people of different ilk! I firmly believed that I was going to enjoy a disease-free, healthy life at least until I was 75 or 80. So the question tortured me -- "Why did this happen to me?"

During the next several days I found the answer after a lot of reading, searching and contemplating. Just as an archaeologist finds more and more ancient relics and artefacts as he digs deeper and deeper, I discovered several reasons and explanations of my heart attack.

Labouring under an illusion that they posed no danger to me, I had become blind to the warning signs. There were two major risk factors -- I am a male and my age was over 40. These were unavoidably part and parcel of mine. In addition, I had developed diabetes a couple of years earlier. Diabetics carry an extra risk of atherosclerosis (narrowing of blood vessels). This is caused by an increase in the amount of cholesterol in the blood. The cholesterol deposits form a layer on the inner linings of major blood vessels, effectively narrowing the blood passages. My blood cholesterol level had reached 244 milligrams.

Now, if you have your blood tested for cholesterol, the pathologist's report will most likely say that the 'normal' level of blood cholesterol is 150 to 240 mg. My cholesterol level was very close to this 'normal' level. How could it be construed as a risk factor?

My reading led me to realise that I had grossly misunderstood the meaning of this word 'normal'. As applied to the blood cholesterol level, 'normal' does not, by any stretch of imagination, imply desirable, ideal or physical wellness. It is a technical term in statistics, to describe what is observed in the majority of people. When a large number of Americans were tested for their blood cholesterol level, it exhibited a bell shaped curve called 'normal distribution'. The cholesterol levels of nearly 95% of the population lay between 150 and 240 mg. It does not mean that the blood cholesterol level of a healthy person should be between 150 and 240. A large number of Americans who suffer from heart attack belong to the population whose blood cholesterol level lies between 150 and 240 mg and it is a top-ranking killer in America. And, in medical profession, we had been mistakenly equating normal with desirable, optimum. We believed that a blood cholesterol level between 150 and 240 was normal, as if it were a clean bill of health! We had confused a descriptive level to be a prescriptive norm. And we had been advising our patients to make sure that their blood cholesterol level lay between 150 and 240. It is clear to me now that by doing so, we were telling our patients that by keeping the blood cholesterol level between 150 and 240, they would be just as likely to suffer heart attack as an average American!

The world famous 'Framingham Study', which was started after the Second World War and which still continues, during the last fifty years of observation, showed that no one whose blood cholesterol level was below 150 mg had suffered a heart attack. The probability of a heart attack increased as the blood cholesterol level increased above 150 mg. Reading this made me realise that all these years my blood cholesterol level, 244 mg, was well above the 'risk level' though I was under an illusion that it was 'normal', and safe!

Why should my blood cholesterol level have increased? I knew that the blood cholesterol level increases in those who eat meat, those who smoke, those who are obese, those who have sedentary habits and therefore lack proper physical exercise, those who must cope with mental stress and those whose life style is highly competitive. I did not belong to any of these groups. My diet was one hundred percent vegetarian. But, in our family, my mother, my aunts and my grandmother had nothing but praise for milk and milk products. Since childhood I had developed a fondness for milk and fatty milk products such as ghee (clarified butter). My grandmother always forwarded the example of her father -- my great grandfather. Nearly a hundred years earlier, he was a landlord in a village in Khandesh, one of the divisions of the state of Maharashtra. Once his house was attacked at night by a band of robbers, who had come armed with swords. My great grandfather had no weapons and was alone at home. He had a strong physique. As the fiends climbed upstairs to grab hold of my great grandfather, he climbed to the third floor of his house and noticed, nearly 30 feet below, his horse standing on the ground. Without a moment's hesitation, he jumped on the back of the horse and single handed broke the siege of the gangsters and escaped.

My grandmother must have told me a countless number of times that my great grandfather used to consume a small bowl of ghee during the course of every meal and that is why he was so strong. She insisted that we children must also consume milk and ghee, and lots of it. Once I started attending the medical college I read these scientific facts. Whenever I told my grandmother that eating ghee was unsafe for health, she would outright reject my scientific reasoning and would cite the irrefutable example of her father. I had no answer to that. A few of years before she passed away, when she was about 100 years old, I asked her how old my great grandfather was when he died. She said, "He died when he was 32. He had a sudden chest pain while he was eating his meal, his head drooped to one side and before anything could be done, he was gone!" Certainly my great grandfather had died of a massive heart attack. I realised too well what can happen if you consume a bowl of ghee at every meal.

Since then I reduced my consumption of ghee. But I had not controlled my fondness for milk. Also, I loved sweets and ice cream. Most animal products such as milk, butter, ghee, animal flesh, eggs and some others such as chocolates and coconut oil contain huge amounts of cholesterol. The dairy products that I consumed must have contributed to the high cholesterol level in my blood.

One often hears a lay argument that there is no connection between fatty foods and heart trouble, because "so and so eats lots of fatty foods, but has not suffered from a heart disease". Another common adage is that in the good old days, people consumed a lot of milk, butter and ghee, but nothing ever happened to them.

And indeed, one does observe that such statements are not entirely untrue. My grandmother, who lived to be 107, regularly consumed milk and ghee, although we had never measured her cholesterol level. My mother is also a devoted fan of milk and ghee. But her cholesterol has not increased to unsafe levels. In fact, her HDL is close to 60! Extremely safe! On the other hand, there is my great grandfather who had passed away long before I was born. He consumed lots of ghee every day, probably had a very high cholesterol level and died of a massive heart attack at the age of 32. And in the end, there was I! So, in one family, we see different pictures in four consecutive generations. Why?

The cells of liver remove the low-density lipids (LDL), i.e. the undesirable portion of cholesterol, from the blood. The ability of liver to remove LDL from the blood stems from the presence of 'LDL receptors' on liver cells. And the number of such receptors on the surface of liver cells is determined by heredity.

If your liver cells carry a large number of LDL receptors, then the liver can very effectively remove LDL from the blood, thus nullifying the effect of the fatty foods you consume. Most probably, my mother and my grandmother had inherited this ability. Even when they consumed high-fat diets, their cholesterol did not increase to unsafe levels. On the other hand, people with few LDL receptors, (for instance my great grandfather and myself); will see a dangerous rise in their cholesterol. Thus, the same high-fat diet affects different people differently, depending upon the number of LDL receptors on their liver cells. Since one does not know which group one belongs to, a safe gamble is to avoid the high-fat diets and to thereby keep the LDL levels low. If your total blood cholesterol level is exceeding 150 mg, you should know that your liver cells cannot filter out the cholesterol load you are consuming.

That in the old days people were not adversely affected by a diet rich in milk and milk products like butter and ghee is not entirely true. Many, like my great grandfather, probably died young. I do not think anyone kept a count. Rani's two uncles died of heart attack in their 30s. Both were landlords, they ate sumptuous meals. There must have been many like them. Those who died young were forgotten. We see the ones that lived on (survival basis) and draw a wrong conclusion that health is not affected by high-fat diets. Similar wrong argument is sometimes forwarded for smoking as well. 'The cigar smoker, Winston Churchill lived till he was 81!'

The high-density lipid (HDL) portion of cholesterol also exerts its protective influence. My HDL count was very low, around 30. My mother's HDL count is 61 while one of my friends has an HDL level of 71. Obviously, they face a substantially lower risk of heart trouble. Raising one's HDL level is a tough task. Regular exercise helps but I did not exercise. Hence my HDL level had slipped to a low value. Despite the doubly dangerous levels of LDL and HDL cholesterol for years, I carried an illusion of immunity from heart diseases and kept on indulging my taste for milk and sweets.

Besides, how much hard physical labour the people in the old days did! Walking 10 to 15 kilometres a day, fetching water from a long distance, milking of cattle, chopping the wood and farmer's chores was a regular part of life. Large joint families and the close bonds with clan, tribe, caste or the village community, the non-competitive, contented attitude these all provided protection from a heart attack. They could eat a fat rich diet and yet remain safe. "But not you, my dear!"

1.6

Medical science knows that lack of exercise and a sedentary occupation increase the risk of heart disease. Though I worked amongst the aborigines in Gadchiroli, my work did not involve any physical labour. I had no time for regular exercise. The 24 hours of a day were not enough to accomplish what I wanted to do. Reading was important to me, examining the patients was necessary, and social work and research were my primary responsibilities. To run an institution, to meet a hundred to two hundred people a day, to carefully read piles of paper each day, to give lectures and to participate in meetings and to be on the run all the time -- these were all important activities for me. But what about my body? It did hunger for food, but it did not ask for physical labour and exercise. And even if it asked for it, I did not listen to it. I used to exercise regularly till I was 17. I used to play football (soccer). But, once I entered the medical college as a student, my exercise stopped. Since that time, for the last 27 years, I had not exercised on a regular basis. It was significant that I had stopped exercising after joining the medical college. As if I had assumed that from then on, the physicians and hospitals would take care of me; I had the liberty to be absolutely irresponsible. Why did I need exercise? I was in a medical college!

But then, does body really need exercise at all? To be honest, I have felt a certain dislike and apathy towards any kind of physical labour since my childhood. And indeed, why should one have to engage in any form of hard physical labour in this age of machines? Intellectual activity having assumed a high level of importance, physical labour seems to have been banished from the lifestyle of the educated class. The messy experience of sweating profusely from a hard physical chore pales in comparison to the delights of watching television or reading a book while comfortably seated in an easy chair. One instinctively recoils from the prospect of pain and sweat.

The Indian society, in general, looks down upon physical labour. From the creation of the lowest social class of *shudras* thousands of years back and burdening it with hard physical chores to the creation of a class of white-collar *babus* in modern India, this disdain for physical labour is seen among Indians everywhere. A recent study showed that the children of Indian immigrants in the UK play or exercise less than their White or Black peers.

But what harm could a lack of exercise possibly cause? During the last ten-fifteen years scientists have uncovered some startling facts. Due to the lack of physical exercise the human body cells do not respond too well to the hormone 'insulin'. This has been called insulin resistance. That leads to an increase in the blood sugar. In other words, it leads to diabetes. In order to compensate for the reduced response to insulin, the body secretes more insulin. A chronic (ever present) surplus of insulin leads to narrowing of blood vessels, increase in blood pressure, increase in cholesterol, atherosclerosis, and finally to a heart disease. Medical scientists call this entire cluster of abnormalities 'Syndrome X' or 'Metabolic Syndrome'.

However, Dr. George Sheehan, a renowned expert from the USA, calls this litany of ailments by the name 'Exercise Deficiency Disease'. Just as a lack of vitamins causes specific diseases, a lack of physical activity and exercise causes 'Exercise Deficiency Disease'. While the high blood pressure, diabetes, high cholesterol and heart disease -- all occur silently inside the body, the only external manifestation is the collection of fat over abdomen. This presents itself in the form of increased girth of abdomen – the so-called 'central obesity'. The circumference of waist becomes larger than the circumference of one's hips. A large number of well-to-do people of Indian origin, either in India or abroad, are today suffering from Syndrome X. I was one such example of Syndrome X!

1.7

One more illusion was dispelled while I lay in the hospital bed. For the past seventeen years, I had been working to improve the health of rural and tribal people in Maharashtra. If asked, "What are the major diseases of the Indian society at large?" the answer will include malnutrition, anaemia, tuberculosis, leprosy, malaria, dysentery, typhoid, pneumonia and so on. By contrast, heart disease is perceived as being common amongst the Westerners and the wealthy upper classes. I had never perceived heart disease as a major problem in India. But when I was diagnosed with angina, I began to recollect.

A brother-in-law of mine, professor of Management in a college, suffered a fatal heart attack only a few days ago, at the age of 53. A cousin of mine, 55 years old, a sales manager in one company, had a heart attack and passed away two years ago. Tushar Khorgade, one of our colleagues in SEARCH, broke the news that his brother-in-law had suffered a heart attack. How old do you think he was? 37! Vivek, my nephew, was six or seven years younger than me. When he was a little boy, I used to delight him by carrying him around on my shoulders. He grew up to be a handsome, vivacious young man full of joy and gusto. Used to run a farm in the jungle land in another state, Madhya Pradesh. Vivek suddenly died of heart attack at the age of 37! And, while I was writing all this, we received the news that my cousin sister's husband passed away -- heart attack at the age of 46!

It was an unwelcome consolation that almost every educated middle class person who came to see me in the hospital had at least one close relative in his family who had suffered a heart attack. Many of my visitors themselves or members of their families had undergone a bypass surgery. I was witnessing an unexpected but new phenomenon. Heart attack was striking in India at a progressively younger age. When I was a medical student, we used to consider heart attack as a disease occurring after the age of 60. But now I was seeing heart attack strike people in their 50s, 40s and even 30s! One of my classmates at the medical school had his first bypass surgery at the age of 28! I said “first surgery” because he underwent his second bypass surgery recently!

“What on earth is going on? Why are these people, the ‘cream of the society’, dying of heart attack at such a young age? Is there an epidemic of coronary heart disease in India?” I wondered.

Surveys of men over 40 years in Delhi and Chennai found that one in five had diabetes and one in ten had a coronary heart disease. No other population sample in the world has shown an evidence of such a high proportion of people suffering from these two ailments. Many such surveys conducted in India since 1970 have shown that the proportion of men suffering from diabetes and/or heart disease is on the increase. Every decade there is an increase in the proportion of people with heart disease or diabetes and the age at which these diseases occurred progressively decreased. Now an Indian male faces death by the time he reaches his 30s or 40s. I was one such male.

Nearly fifty years ago, the USA witnessed a similar wave of coronary heart disease. The economy was booming after the end of the Second World War, the standard of living had gone up, there was plenty of food for every one and the machines had just about eliminated the need for any hard physical labour. Some people have dubbed this new American lifestyle as a ‘lifestyle revolving around the triad of car, TV and supermarket’. The automobile eliminated the need for walking. People sat in front of a TV and watched entertainment too frequently punctuated by commercials, drove their cars to supermarkets, bought everything they saw in the commercials and ate those things again sitting in front of a TV. Due to this lifestyle, the number of people in the USA who suffered and died from heart diseases considerably increased during the decade from 1950 to 1960. During the next ten or fifteen years, the Americans found the underlying factors to be smoking, diet rich in animal fats (milk, butter, cheese, eggs and meat), increased levels of blood cholesterol and exercise-less lifestyle. An exercise-less lifestyle was recognised as a risky lifestyle. An office, a chair, a drawing room, a sofa and a bedroom are the most dangerous places, because a large majority of people in affluent nations die in these places. With this realisation, the American society began to make conscious changes in lifestyle.

What happened in the USA fifty years ago is happening in India today. A large class of well-to-do people has arisen in India. The upper middle class and the middle class together make up 300 million people in India today and that is nearly as many people as the population of entire USA! This 'America in India' is rapidly learning and internalising the American lifestyle-rich food, freedom from physical labour, alcohol and smoking. The automobile, TV, refrigerator and restaurants promoting eating out have come to dominate the modern life. It is cultivating a culture that de-emphasizes exercise and physical labour and emphasizes gluttonous eating. And along with that there is a rising ambition fed by a tremendous competition in career. Given the busy schedules and deadlines that rule their careers with an iron hand, it is no wonder the upper middle class and middle class people in India are experiencing mental stress that is no different than the one that the Westerners face. That is why we are seeing such an increase in heart diseases amongst the Indians.

But there must be something more, hidden, to cause this huge epidemic. Indians seem to be much more vulnerable to coronary heart diseases than the Westerners that have adopted a lifestyle of conspicuous consumption. Thousands of Indians have now settled in the UK, Singapore, Canada, South Africa and the USA. A vast majority of these Indians has attained the middle class or even the upper middle class standard of living in those countries. Their lifestyle is deeply influenced by the wealth of those countries. When comparative studies were conducted in the UK on the White, Black and Indians with more or less similar lifestyles, the medical scientists found that the incidence of diabetes and heart disease was highest in the people of Indian origin. When the parents and grandparents of these Indians lived in rural India, diabetes and heart disease were relatively rare amongst them. However, on adopting the lifestyle of well-to-do Westerners, they proved to be far more vulnerable than the Westerners -- White or Black!

The same picture was found in Singapore, South Africa and Canada. And it is now emerging in urban India too. It is now an established opinion of the medical science that there must be some genetic or intra-uterine factors that predispose Indians to diabetes and heart diseases. The explanation of the wave of heart diseases in India thus lies in the unfortunate combination of genetic predisposition and the new lifestyle of the middle and the upper classes in India.

1.8

In spite of all these factors, I did not feel that I completely understood the cause of my sickness. Why should a person, who was not driven by the lure of money or by a highly competitive career, who lived in a rural settlement of aborigines, who found happiness in providing health care and carried out his own research at his own pace, who lived a life free of intense desires and stress, develop heart disease?

A search for the cause of my malady was a delicate task. Was I really free of desires and stress? If I were, then why did I not feel at peace with myself for the last few years? Indeed, I did not feel joyful for the past four or five years. Life felt tasteless the way a person with fever finds food tasteless. I must confess that I was feeling sad and frustrated in some strange, indescribable way for the last few years. It was as if the very essence of life was lost. Why? And whence? My mind began to search.

When I was in my 20s, I participated actively in the campaigns for social and political reform led by Jayaprakash Narayan and Vinoba Bhave[4], eminent national leaders and followers of Mahatma Gandhi.

---

4. *Vinoba Bhave, considered to be the spiritual heir of Mahatma Gandhi, was a saint-philosopher, a polyglot who knew 27 languages, a great master of the Gita and Hindu philosophy. He founded his Bhoodan campaign to bring about a peaceful revolution in the ownership of land in India. He walked the length and breadth of India and persuaded many landlords to donate land to desperately poor peasants, so that they could till the land and be self-sufficient. He led the followers of Gandhi – the Sarvodaya Movement – for nearly 25 years after Gandhi's death.*

Life was blooming in every direction. After receiving the degree of M.D. I married Rani and plunged into social work. We were going to change the society for better! We had an intoxicating altruistic dream and I felt 'high' all the time. Success, or no success, the joy of devoting one's self completely for a larger cause was so intense that no sacrifice seemed enough. Our feelings were aptly expressed in the immortal lines of the famous Marathi poet Kusumagraj --

With our own hands we laid
The fiery path of burning coals
And on and on we madly rushed
Down the path to the cherished goals.

Where from, then, did this unease arise? We were in our early 30s when Rani and I went to the USA for higher education. The time we spent at the Johns Hopkins University was a period of pure intellectual ecstasy. Students from 77 different countries, world-renowned professors and a constant pursuit of knowledge gave one a real rush. Academically, I was a top notcher. Our professors were sure that Rani and I were destined to accomplish something really special in the field of public health. My heart was brimming with pure joy and eager anticipation. Where from, then, did this sadness arise?

When we returned to India, we founded our organisation SEARCH in the district of Gadchiroli. The next few years passed swiftly as we buried ourselves in providing health care to aborigines, researching the health problems the Indian villages faced, reducing child mortality, campaigning for the control of alcoholic beverages in these rural areas and developing the beautiful campus of Shodhagram for SEARCH. Work increased way beyond our abilities to handle it. We built a hospital for the aborigines. Our research on health problems in rural areas earned us a national and international recognition. We succeeded in getting alcohol legally banned in Gadchiroli. SEARCH became a benchmark in the arena of community health in India. But what was happening to me while all this happened?

I began to peep into the cave of memory, and to re-live that period of ten years. Soon after this phase of my life had begun, the sense of joy had slowly begun to fade. I began to lose the sense of peace and well-being. Why? I had forced upon myself something unnatural, something that was not my own self. And the inner change I had begun to experience was a reaction to this unnaturalness, this not-me-ness of whatever I was forcing upon myself. What was this unnatural thing? What was this 'not-me' thing?

Soon after we founded SEARCH in Gadchiroli, we also made an attempt, in deference to frequent requests from the state government of Maharashtra, to improve the government run health care system, which included the district hospital and a primary health care centre. During that early period, we had to face and to cope with the red tape-ism in the government, incorrigible tendency to prevent doing anything or allowing others to do anything worthwhile, extreme delays, unimaginable laziness, corruption and even Machiavellian scheming to brand us as criminals. For two years we felt as if we were allowing a hideous worm to crawl and slither all over our bodies. Finally, we disengaged ourselves from it, but several scars remained. For two years we had been immeasurably unjust to ourselves. Did that cause this sense of unwell-being? But it should have disappeared once we disengaged ourselves. What happened after that?

The deeper I thought about this, the scarier I felt. An abscess had developed deep in my mind; it was throbbing with pus, was ready for being incised. But I was hesitant, afraid to take the final step, but it had to be taken. I had to explore myself and accept what I had begun to recognise as the truth even if it was frighteningly painful. What happened next? Why did I lose my peace of mind?

As our work in Gadchiroli kept on expanding, my own self, the very I-ness of mine, changed too. This highly successful I was quite different from the natural I. They drifted further and further apart and increased my stress. As our initial research on the health of the rural people in Gadchiroli became successful, instead of bringing me happiness and peace, the horizons of expectation shifted further away. I felt an eagerness to see the results of our research implemented nationwide and even worldwide, to see the measures to control alcohol introduced in Gadchiroli applied to the entire state of Maharashtra. And to make this happen, I was simultaneously operating at two different levels. On one level I was living among the aborigines of Gadchiroli. On the other level, I was living the life of an intellectual, a scientist, among the policy makers in Mumbai, Delhi, London and New York. 'I' was stretched like a rubber. This experience was highly stressful; the work itself was a joyless dollop of pure starch. But I had accepted it as a temporary phase, thinking that it will lead to something useful for society. But no end was in sight to what I had accepted only as a 'temporary' situation.

As time went on, my sense of altruism was getting mixed with personal ambition. I was fired by the passion for success. I was determined to reach 'somewhere'. I did not know where! And so, no matter where I reached during my journey, I found no satisfaction of having 'arrived'. There was a persistent, compelling feeling that what I wanted to achieve was quite different from what I had actually accomplished. There was a constant feeling that a very different, unique 'something' was going to happen in my life and I was anxious for 'it' to happen. There was a persistent dissatisfaction and an ever-present yearning. My own work was no longer a spring of joy. It had become a means of some external success and, therefore, a source of inner dissatisfaction. Until this stage in my life, I was working for the social betterment, and was least concerned about the rewards and personal gains, and yet, experienced a sense of pure bliss. And now, I was working for the results, for the fruits it might bear; I had lost that earlier joy and peace!

Now emotions were replaced by thoughts, by rational thinking. I had divorced myself from the emotional richness of my experiences and had turned every experience, into an intellectual activity. Gradually I had lost touch with my feelings. I did not feel; instead, I thought about my feelings. Instead of living fully each moment of my life, I had begun to think about it. For last many years I had forgotten the joyful notes of music and tidal sweeps of literature. Exiled from the luscious world of emotions, my mind experienced the depressing pathos of sad emptiness. This in itself was not a disease; it was only a warning sign. But I was ignoring this danger signal emanating from deep within me. And that is why the stress level had increased till it became unbearable. Did that stress and depression turn into my heart disease?

My friend Dr. Anita Awchat sent me a book to read while I was confined in the hospital. It was the famous book '*Love, Medicine and Miracle*' by an American surgeon Dr. Bernie Siegal. He has written how cancer patients were treated with sheer will power and mind exercises. He says that our mind exerts a tremendous influence on our body. Many cancer patients were found to have suffered bouts of depression before the onset of cancer. Depression, anxiety and fear send negative messages to the body and the living cells lose both the will and the ability to live on. Then cancer or some other equally menacing sickness gains a stranglehold on the body. A body engrossed in anxiety and negative emotions allows these diseases to take root and to grow. There is no will left to fight against these diseases. I felt that Bernie Siegal's views could be valid.

And recently I came across a research paper that supports Bernie Siegal's hypothesis. Lately, scientists have developed a technique for measuring the degree of atherosclerosis. Using this technique, scientists in Berkley, California examined the major blood vessels of various individuals. Blood vessels of those who were sad and depressed were found to be unusually narrowed and constricted compared to the blood vessels of the rest of the people. Sadness and depression do indeed lead to heart disease!

1.9

Dr. Shervitz and Dr. Powel have reported an extremely interesting observation. They recorded the normal conversations of heart disease patients and counted the number of times words like

'I', 'Me', 'Mine', 'to me' occurred. Those who were overly preoccupied with their own selves manifesting as more frequent use of self-related words, subsequently suffered from recurrence of heart disease more frequently.

So this 'I' seems to be very treacherous. Toxic to the heart! But why?

Anything that isolates one from the rest of the world brings on loneliness and hence stress, which finally leads to heart disease. On the other hand, things that promote love and bonding, things that link up an individual with nature and with the Universe, protect the heart. In fact, scientific studies have shown that emotional bonding not only with other people, but also with pets and even with trees can protect people from heart disease.

According to Erich Fromm, one of the most eminent psychologists after Sigmund Freud, a relationship is not just something human being desires, but is a basic need of human beings for living. In the self-centred and competitive modern civilisation, an individual is left alone, lonely and alienated from the rest of the world. An individual in such a civilisation remains lonely in a crowd and a combative adversary of everyone else. I versus the whole world! Just as one must be a fierce competitor in one's professional life out there in the world, one also brings the spirit of competition indoors; husband and wife vie for the same role, power, status and domination. And finally, one competes against one's own self in pursuit of greater success. This combative competition generates an ever-present stress. It snips away the relationships with others. To survive in such a civilisation, one must constantly chant the mantra of 'I' and 'Mine'. 'I' becomes the most important idol worshipped day and night.

I remembered a tale Acharya Rajaneesh used to tell during his discourses. Once a dog, who was a highly respected spiritual guru in the kingdom of dogs, started on a journey from Calcutta to Delhi on foot. His disciples in Calcutta bid him a gala farewell. He was scheduled to reach Delhi in three months. His followers, in anticipation of his arrival in Delhi after three months, organised a committee to plan a grand reception ceremony. The committee started a fund raising campaign for this reception. But before they could even print the receipt books for fund raising, the great guru dog arrived in Delhi in only ten days after leaving Calcutta. His surprised followers were full of admiration for the master. “Long live Dog the Great!”, they shouted.

“Sir, how did you accomplish this miracle of travelling from Calcutta to Delhi in mere ten days? And how did you get all those bruises?” they asked.

“I did not make this journey so rapidly of my own accord”, answered the Great one. “After leaving Calcutta, I walked many miles. When I made my first stop, I was tired and hungry. But, as soon as I entered that town, all the dogs there started barking at me furiously. They started chasing me. With a pounding heart I ran fast. When I reached the next town, I was hopeful that I could rest there for a while and catch my breath. But the dogs in that town were even more vicious. They sank their teeth in my flesh! And that is the secret of my rapid journey. I was not allowed to stop and rest anywhere between Calcutta and Delhi!” The Great One, crying and panting, blurted out.

Competition in today’s world is like this kind of running fast and ‘reaching Delhi’. Is this called ‘success’!

I have heard that ‘Dog the Great’ soon died of a heart attack!

For the competitive economy to succeed, selfishness, greed and ambition need to be fired up in the heart of every individual in the society and that fire needs to be constantly fed. The lethal dash for ‘advancement’, propelled by sheer selfishness and greed, generates an intense stress, which leads to heart disease. This fate awaits not only those who lead a competitive life in big cities like Mumbai, Pune and Nagpur, but even a social worker providing medical care in the forest of Gadchiroli had not been able to escape it.

In the Oscar-winning role in the movie “*On the Waterfront*”, Marlon Brando says something that I found very fascinating: “Charlie ... I could have been somebody"! It shows a yearning to become something or someone other than who and what I am right now. I *am* somebody in this instant, but I find no satisfaction in it. I have no relation with that somebody. I am sad that I am not someone different, someone else. I chase that mirage and let my own relationship with myself snap off.

This desire to become 'a big shot', to become 'successful' is motivated by the innate need to prove that I am different from the others, more significant than others, more endowed than others. To be like others is to become 'common'. To become 'uncommon', I need to become different. I need to emphasize, not my commonality, but what is unique to me to differentiate myself from others. I start building a wall of my uniqueness around myself and thus become a lonely prisoner inside. This self-inflicted solitary confinement turns dangerous and fatal to the heart.... Suddenly I began to see clearly the reason for my own illness!

Sometime many years ago, unknowingly, imperceptibly, I had handed over my healthy way of life and my cheerful mind to this modern civilisation. First I stopped exorcising my body and began to ignore its needs. Then I began to run after 'success', became a workaholic and somewhere in that pursuit lost my state of blissfulness. In the desert of intellect and reasoning, I became alienated from my own feelings. As time went on, the preoccupation with 'I' and 'Mine' kept on increasing. It became a barbed wire fence and I lost the feeling of oneness with the people, and then with the Universe. And surprisingly, with the loss of my oneness with the world, I lost the touch with my own self. I had lost relationship with my own self. I had lost my own home. My integral, whole, healthy life had shattered. I was broken into pieces. All this while, one internal organ, a compass, was trying to alert me that something was terribly wrong. But I kept ignoring it, kept on pushing ahead. I believe that this loss of relationship with my own self-created the stress and depression, which most probably led to my heart disease.

It was not my heart alone that was sick. I was sick! The whole of me! And now I was in this hospital as a patient!

1.10

One day Rani came in fuming with anger. The lift operator of the hospital had demanded to see her 'visitor pass'. Since she had not carried that pass along, the lift operator had asked her to step out of the lift. My room was on the third floor of the hospital. Without the lift, there was no other way for her to come and see me. She was torn between anxiety for me and the insult she felt due to the lift operator's rude refusal. Of course the lift operator's refusal had the support of hospital rules. But, up until now, both Rani and I had always moved about in hospitals as physicians. Today, our roles had changed. I was a patient and Rani was a patient's relative, a visitor. And it was our turn now to taste what patients and patients' relatives must feel in hospitals.

The word 'hospital' comes from a Latin word, which means a 'guest'. Hospitality includes everything that makes a guest feel welcome. But the construction of hospitals often does not reflect the spirit of hospitality. Take a hospital ward for example. To make it easy for a doctor or a nurse to keep an eye on all patients at one glance, thirty or forty sick, moaning, weeping and barely clad patients are kept in one hall, with no respect for their pain, privacy or the need for peaceful and quiet sleep. A jail warden wants such an arrangement to see all the prisoners at one glance and so does a cattle herder! Indeed, to understand why the aborigines in Shodhagram liked our idea of building a hospital of separate huts where a patient and his or her relatives could be housed, one has to become a patient!

After a week had passed without any 'event', Dr. Bidwai decided to discharge me from the hospital. Rani brought my discharge card. I read the words "DM with IHD" written on it in bold letters and felt like a red hot iron had burned a brand on my chest. It was an abbreviation of my ailments -- Diabetes Mellitus with Ischemic Heart Disease. I knew my diagnosis, but after seeing my discharge card I realised for the first time that I had become a permanent member of the crowd of thousands of faceless patients. Until now, I had almost mechanically stamped these letters on the papers of hundreds of my patients. I had never been aware of how the patients themselves felt after receiving their own diagnosis. To us, the physicians, diagnosis and treatment were purely intellectual activities, not emotional investments. Our diagnosis was an intellectual feat, very much like Sherlock Holmes solving the riddle of a murder. What did Sherlock Holmes know about how the murdered person might have felt? It was the least of his concerns. We had never experienced a patient's illness on an emotional plane. Today I began to understand a lot of things after becoming a patient.

We moved to Rani's brother's home in Nagpur. I was kept on the ground floor in that two-storey house, so that I would not have to go up and down the staircase. As if my heart had become fragile like glass!

While I was recuperating, many people came to see me. As I looked at them, my mind did calculations -- "How old would this man be? Maybe 55? How much longer would he live? At least 20 years. How lucky is he! I am not assured of even a few days!" I found myself envying everyone for the assurance of the years of life he or she seemed to carry. I was bargaining for each day!

Whenever a friend or a relative was leaving me, I felt a pang. I may never see him or her again. This might very well be our last meeting. I used to bid them a silent farewell in my mind.

Some visitors used to bring a breeze of cheer. They used to make me laugh, assure me that everything would be all right. My mind used to forget the throbbing awareness of impending danger. "Perhaps, I would indeed survive this sickness just as these people are saying."

But many others would come in with sombre expressions on their faces, as if it were a cultural tradition not to appear cheerful when visiting a sick person! They would sit with me and mirror all the pain and anxiety I was feeling inside. They would speak to me in barely audible whispers. I could read the grim question written on their faces. They would tell me the tales of how someone closely related to them suddenly died of heart attack. As they left my room, they would make it a point to remind me, "Be very careful. This is a very dangerous sickness, there is no guarantee of survival from it". "They just completed the duty of performing my last rites!" I used to think.

Rani's father, Dr. Chari came to see me. I am his youngest son-in-law. We call him Bawa. He was a very popular 'family doctor' in Chandrapur, a small district town. He is 71 years old and has now retired from his medical practice. He has recently been diagnosed with cancer, was taken to the UK where it was decided at the end of all tests, to not subject him to any treatment. He has limited life to live.

Bawa showed no sign of sickness or worry. He talks to me in make-do Hindi because I do not speak Telugu and he does not speak Marathi. But his talk was very amusing. He said, "Abhay, I know I have to go soon. So what is the point in wasting time in crying? And why fear cancer? Every one dies of this or that illness. It is good that I now have the label of cancer. Otherwise I would die without any cause!"

Bawa's attitude has not ceased to amaze me. This man does not read any spiritual books or books on philosophy. All his life he examined and treated patients with tender loving care, took care of his family and fully enjoyed the warmth of the company of people in Chandrapur.

His love for people and his desire to meet people are strange and strong. He lives these days with his son in Nagpur, but every now and then he slips out of Nagpur and boards a bus to Chandrapur. He is a stranger in Nagpur. Chandrapur is his place. And he prefers to ride a bus to going in a car his son owns. He says, "If I travel by car, whom would I meet? When I ride a bus, I meet thirty or forty people in one trip!"

"From where does he get this irrepressible courage and all-pervading love?" In my mind I saluted my father-in-law and said, "Bawa, please give me a piece of your strange spirituality. I am in great need of it."

One of my friends is a physician. He came to see me. We have been buddies since we were in the medical school. A love for music and books of P. L. Deshpande, a gifted Marathi littérateur, brought us together forever. In the medical school we spent a lot of time together organising music concerts. Now he had come to find me lying in a hospital as a heart patient. He did not say much. After he left, his mother told me that he had cried like a baby, right in his hospital, when he heard of my heart attack. But when he met me, he made no show of his emotions; he did not let me see his sentimental side.

Some visitors used to bring much happiness with them. Our friend Ranjan Darvekar came to see me. Ranjan knows the magic of making people laugh. You never know when he would crack a joke in the midst of a conversation or when his humour would suddenly turn into a philosophical statement. He said to me, "It is a pity you got a heart attack at such a young age. Abhay, you made one blunder. For the last twenty years, you gave your heart to just one girl! Your heart has been stationary in one place and is now rusty! Look at me. I keep my heart moving -- I give it to one girl today, to another tomorrow! That is why my heart has no disease!" And he preached all this right in Rani's presence!

Many friends used to say, "Tell us if you need any help!" They wanted to help, but did not know exactly what they could do to help me. Men do not understand how to care for someone, how to express affection through small talk, small gestures and seemingly insignificant actions. Women are naturally gifted in this department. Men behave very awkwardly and in an unnatural manner at times like this. And if they cannot think of anything, they start talking about politics!

Many visitors were possessed by such a keen curiosity that it appeared to me much stronger than their concern for my health. They would drag me into a discussion about how this disease comes about. They had a full-fledged physician at their disposal to satisfy their curiosity. And as luck would have it, the physician was confined to bed! Well, so far so good. But then they would ask me what complications could possibly occur in this disease and I would have to tell them about all the probable complications. Even that would not satisfy some people's curiosity. "What exactly happens then?", they would ask. Then I had to tell them how one (i.e. me!) could possibly die if the heart stopped beating altogether as a result of the heart disease. Fear and eagerness would shine on their faces as if they were watching a horror movie. Some even asked me, "Now that you do not have any certainty about life, how exactly do you feel?" or "What do you feel like doing in whatever little time you are left with?" Not a word of this is an exaggeration. Sometimes the thought used to cross my mind that one could write describing these strange facets of human behaviour. And immediately my mind would say, "What good is it to me now?"

When no one was around, my mind would once again be possessed by the ever-dreadful basic question. "What will happen?" My mind used to engage itself in the same game of numbers -- "What is the probability of death? What is the probability of my surviving for another year? Would I live for at least five more years? What would I do if I stayed alive?"

1.11

Dr. P.S. Bidwai is one of the senior heart specialists in India. When I was a student, legends of Dr. Bidwai's sharp intellect used to be told in the medical colleges in Nagpur and Chandigarh where he had worked and taught. However, during my stay in the hospital in Nagpur, I repeatedly experienced that his heart was bigger than his intellect. While speaking about what attitude a physician must cultivate, he once said, "If your patient dies, but your eyes do not brim with tears while meeting the patient's family members, you should seriously consider an occupation other than medicine." Dr. Bidwai's attitude was radically different from the commonly advocated and observed cold-blooded norm in the medical field that a physician should remain emotionally uninvolved with the patient.

Dr. Bidwai administered the treadmill test to me after I had completed two weeks. In the second stage of the test it became abundantly clear that my heart was not getting adequate blood supply.

I did have a coronary heart disease! The uncertainty was over. The question now was whether to perform an angioplasty or a bypass surgery. Dr. Bidwai weighed each option carefully and with as much concern and affection as a father would while caring for his child. Dr. Bidwai decided to have an echocardiogram done. Results of the echocardiogram were encouraging. It meant that though the heart was starved of blood supply, no part of the heart muscle was dead. While looking at my echocardiogram Dr. Bidwai drew Rani to aside and exclaimed gleefully like a child, "Rani, it looks like we would not need to perform a bypass surgery on Abhay!" Rani later told me that while I was taking the treadmill test, and when the test results were showing that I had the coronary heart disease, Dr. Bidwai was banging his fist on the table with disappointment. The same Dr. Bidwai was thrilled when the echocardiogram test showed an undamaged heart. Listening to Rani's account brought tears to my eyes. "Why are you getting so much involved in me, Sir?" My heart cried. "I may cause you more pain."

Nagpur did not have advanced facilities. So Dr. Bidwai, Rani and my sister-in-law Padmaja flew with me to Lucknow to the Post-Graduate Institute of Medical Science, where Dr. Bidwai had founded the Cardiology Department some years earlier. Many experts in this department were Dr. Bidwai's students or colleagues. Dr. Mahant, now a famous cardiac surgeon at this institute, was the one to whom I had handed over the charge twenty years ago upon completion of my junior residency in cardiology ward. Dr. Nakul Sinha, a specialist in angioplasty, was going to treat me.

Finally it was May 10. At 8.30 in the morning they carried me on a stretcher to the angiography room. It was an odd feeling. Being a physician examining the patient, I was used to looking down at patients who lay in bed or on a stretcher from a higher position. Today, as I looked up while lying down on the stretcher, people's faces, the room, the ceiling, the lights on the angiography table, the faces of doctors looking down at me, everything appeared different. Everything in my life had turned upside down.

The angiography procedure began. A catheter was inserted in the large blood vessel in my right thigh and it was slowly pushed upward till its tip reached my heart. I was fully conscious and was looking at that advancing catheter on a large screen. Dr. Sinha gently introduced the tip of the angiography catheter into coronary blood vessel that supplies blood to the heart and injected a dye. Like a lightening flashing across the sky, a web of twisting and curving blood vessels appeared on the screen for a moment. The camera snapped that picture. Another injection and again a momentary view of the coronary blood vessels appeared on the monitor screen. Another photograph was taken. In this manner they took pictures from all possible angles on a video film. Then the doctors left me there and hurried to another room to carefully review and evaluate all those pictures.

While we anxiously waited for the verdict, Dr. Nakul Sinha came in and told us that out of the three major vessels that bring blood to the heart, two had a 30% blockage. However, the third had a 95% blockage. That was the one posing a real danger and was responsible for my angina. The cardiologists at the institute proposed to unblock that blood vessel by balloon angioplasty. Just in case a bypass surgery became necessary, Dr. Mahant would be ready to perform that operation.

There was no choice. The heart disease was proved with a 100% certainty and of all the possible measures available today, this was the most appropriate one. Rani signed the consent forms on my behalf. I bid her farewell. Once again I lay down on the angioplasty table. Six heart specialists were working on me. Dr. Bidwai, who had taught all of us, held my hand in his, and sat down next to me.

No anaesthesia was administered to me, nor were my eyes covered up or closed. I was able to watch my heart, its pulsations and lines of electro-cardiogram on the screen in front of me. I watched as the tip of the angioplasty catheter entered my coronary blood vessel and reached the 95% blockage point. It stopped there and started struggling to open up the blood vessel at that point. Almost 80% of the block was removed, but no more. I could see everything. The doctors discussed the strategy among themselves and decided to increase the pressure on the blockage. The pressure was increased to three times. Then to four times, to six times, eight times...

Suddenly everyone became quiet in the room. The doctors' faces were covered with masks, so I could not observe them, but I could see that there was distinct change in their movements. Dr. Bidwai stood up. I could see on the screen that while attempting to remove the last portion of the block, the coronary blood vessel was torn from within. The torn lining was hanging in the blood vessel and was itself causing the obstacle. This was the most dreaded complication in the angioplasty procedure. MY CORONARY ARTERY WAS TORN!

I felt a pit form in my stomach. The moment of death had arrived! I could see on the screen my heart still pulsating. But this could be the last contraction of my heart. It could now stop any moment. I was going to watch my last heart beat and then it was going to stop beating altogether. The last moment of my life had arrived.

I felt an icy fear. All supports had fallen. The last anchor was snapping up. "I am going. The life has been quite good but this is the last moment. I will not be here the next moment. I will be thrown into an unfathomable darkness. What will happen next?"

Like a spring of water gushing forth, I felt a sudden flow of words appear in my mind –

Om! 'That' is infinite. 'This' is infinite.
From the infinite arises the infinite.
Even when infinite is removed from infinite,
what remains is still infinite.
Om! Peace! Peace! Peace!

This was a mystical prayer from *Ishavasya Upanishad*[5], sung an hour before dawn during my childhood in the Sevagram ashram. I had not understood its profound and mystical meaning up until now. Now, it bloomed of its own accord in my mind, its deep meaning began to unfold --

"This universe is infinite and the divine principle pervading this universe is also infinite. Both are absolute and complete. One arises out of the other. The absolute principle remains unchanged, and even on subtraction, the infinity remains undiminished. There is no limit, nor end to this play. I am also a part of this infinity. So I too have no beginning and no end. Where is then a room for fear? Peace!"

I also remembered the scientific explanations about the origin of the Universe. The Universe did not exist billions of years ago. And then a colossal explosion occurred, called 'Big Bang', and that marked the beginning of this Universe. That primordial explosion released an immeasurable amount of energy. The same energy condensed into elementary particles, which coalesced into atoms. From the rearrangements of atoms came about the various chemical elements and also the stars, suns, planets and this earth. As time flowed on, my physical body took shape at one moment on this earth. I am also made of the same elementary particles. Even if this physical body dies today, those elementary particles will remain in this universe. They have no 'death', no 'end'. They may not exist in the form of my present physical body, they will assume another form. But they will remain. They will remain forever. Where then is death? I am immortal in the form of these elementary particles. I am indestructible. I was, I am and I will be. The death of this physical body is nothing more than a change from one arrangement of atoms and molecules into another arrangement. Only a rearrangement! There is no reason to

---

5. *Ishavasya is one of the most sacred of the Upanishads, the ancient Hindu philosophical scriptures. It condenses in only 18 mantras the Advaita Vedanta philosophy. This particular Mantra is called 'Shantimantra', the mantra of peace, which appears in the beginning and at the end of Ishavasya. Ishavasya itself appears as a part of a Veda, called Yajur Veda.*

be sad or afraid. Someone must convey this last experience of mine to people. Death is simply dissolution of one arrangement of atoms and molecules; only a dissolution!

In that very moment, I felt an assurance, a help, a support. I felt the warmth of that help. The fear of death melted. The mind became quiet, peaceful. I was ready for my dissolution.

1.12

The next three or four hours my cardiologists were struggling to repair the torn coronary artery. When their efforts failed, they spliced the torn blood vessel using a one-inch long tubular stent of titanium. It did the job, the blood vessel was re-joined. The flow of blood resumed without any interruption. I had been brought into the angioplasty room at 8.30 am, I was taken off the angioplasty table at 7 pm. My physicians were perspiring with anxiety, but I was watching the entire episode as if it were a game. I was still alive. The dissolution of my body particles had been postponed, at least for now.

I was extremely tired. I lay in my bed at night in the intensive care unit. Tubes dangled from my arms and legs. Flashing lines representing my heart beats appeared and disappeared on the monitor screen. I was still alive. Rani, sitting on a stool and utterly exhausted, had rested her head on the side of my bed and fallen asleep. Suddenly, at 2 am, I felt a pain in my chest. The pain quickly grew in intensity like a gathering storm and spread first over the entire chest and then to my jaw and both the arms. I called out Rani's name. She struggled to get off the stool and called the night shift nurse and the doctor in. By then my pain had become excruciating. Never in my life had I experienced a pain so severe. I looked up at the ECG monitor. The S-T wave had dipped down, the T-wave looked upside down. The beating of my heart had become erratic. There was absolutely no doubt -- on the very first night after the angioplasty, I had suffered a heart attack.

The pain had become unbearable. Rani told me later that my face had turned blue. I looked up at the nurse and the doctor on duty. They both stood stunned and stymied. I was a VIP patient and my life was in danger. That had thrown them in utter confusion. I was writhing with pain, but strangely, this time, I was not afraid. I was detached. The living organism in me had fully awakened. Every cell in my body wanted to live. I realised that I must myself do something immediately.

"Sister, start the oxygen. Put a tablet of nitroglycerine under my tongue..." -- I started giving them instructions rapidly. Rani ran out to ring up Dr. Nakul Sinha. The nurse and the doctor understood me and moved fast. "Record the ECG. We should be able to see later what this attack was..." I told them. They took the ECG and handed it me. The cardiogram showed that chest leads number one and two showed that the heart was receiving insufficient supply of blood. Was it an infarction or just insufficiency? Someone slipped a tablet of nitroglycerine under my tongue. In five minutes I could feel the pain recede and ebb away. In about fifteen minutes, the ECG was back to normal.

The storm had raged and passed. And this time too, my heart had survived. But I had a glimpse of what my future could be even after the angioplasty. I was still far from 'safe'. But at that moment I was utterly exhausted. I wanted a little sleep. I was not going to quit fighting. If I stayed alive in the morning, I was going to keep fighting for my life.

*****

2. Ornish

In order to be a realist, you must believe in miracles.

— David Ben-Gurion

2.1

My angioplasty was performed on May 10. I was discharged from the hospital on May 14. Now, all I could do was to take the medicines regularly and to wait for what may come. I had no control over what might happen in future. I was a patient myself. It was a matter of my life and death, and yet, there was nothing more I could do. There was a 20 percent probability that the coronary artery opened by angioplasty could once again become blocked within a year. And the other two blood vessels that were only partially blocked were lurking to bring on a crisis any time. I had received the warning on the very first night after angioplasty. So the probability of another heart attack weighed heavily on my mind. And that could mean either a sudden death, or, if I received sufficient warning, one more angioplasty or a bypass surgery!

The miracle of modern medicine had given me a new opportunity to live, but had not liberated me from the disease. Medical science said that one in three diabetic patients were likely to die within five years even after angioplasty. It left me with no other recourse but to keep on taking my medicines and to anxiously wait for the 35 per cent probability of dying. The limitations of my treatment and this feeling of helplessness were infuriating. I wanted to live, but the grim probabilities facing me were depressing. All the books on heart disease mention that those heart disease patients who become depressed often die; those who remain optimistic survive. Yes, I wanted to live, but where do I find the hope?

As luck would have it, one book reached me when I was in the hospital. This book, '*Reversing Heart Disease*', written by an

American doctor named Dean Ornish, was quite popular in the USA those days. Nearly three months prior to my heart attack, I had placed an order for that book purely out of my interest in medical literature. It fell in my hands when I was a heart disease patient in the hospital! I started reading it avidly while I lay in the hospital bed. This book gave me, not only a hope, but also an assurance, that I could indeed survive my heart disease. This book brought revolutionary change in my subsequent treatment.

Dr. Ornish's treatment is based on the rationale that a heart disease is a result of one's lifestyle. Medicines and surgery do not strike at the root causes; they merely provide a temporary relief from the symptoms. Since the root causes of the disease continue to remain in the patient's life, coronary blood vessels tend to become obstructed again even after angioplasty or bypass surgery. Moreover, these procedures are expensive. So, in order to strike at the root causes of the heart disease, Dr. Ornish suggests the following constellation of measures:

1. Vegetarian diet. Less than 10% of the total caloric intake should come from fats and the intake of cholesterol should be reduced to zero.
2. No smoking; no alcohol.
3. Regular exercise to the body and yogic postures.
4. Deep relaxation by way of '*shavasan*' (a yogic posture of lying down like a corpse) '*pranayam*' (conscious and controlled breathing) and a change in mental attitude.
5. Getting in touch with one's own feelings and developing emotional relationship with others around you.
6. Practising meditation, and search for the spiritual roots and the purpose of life.

There is no dearth of those who loudly advertise their own therapies and claim huge successes. Everywhere in India one comes across professionals as well as amateurs, who confidently advise you to follow their own brands of infallible treatments. Since their claims are often highly exaggerated and most often unfounded, I am very sceptical about them. Dr. Ornish, on the other hand, had tested the validity of his hypothesis scientifically and had gathered irrefutable evidence. When computerised coronary angiograms and PET scans of heart disease patients treated by Dr. Ornish were examined by unbiased physicians 'before' and 'after' his treatment, it was found that obstructions in coronary arteries of 82% of patients had reduced. This evidence was medically sound and statistically valid. Moreover, in the words of one of Dr. Ornish's patients, "Not only did my coronary blood vessels open, but my heart opened, I opened up and the entire life became joyful!" Indeed, little would be gained if only the disease was 'cured', but the patient's life remained joyless. In Dr. Ornish's own words, "This is not merely a treatment of heart disease, but a programme of changing the entire lifestyle of the patient".

Ornish's own story is also worth reading. He was a brilliant student in high school. He wanted to become a medical doctor, but suffered a nervous breakdown under the stress of studies and intense competition. He became depressed, began to contemplate suicide. Having lost all hope he left the college and stayed home, vegetating.

His sister was learning yoga from an Indian swami. With nothing better to do, Ornish also went there, learned yoga and practised it. Within fifteen days he began to feel much better. Since then he was drawn to yoga and Indian lifestyle. He finished his college education and joined the Harvard Medical School. He kept up with yogic practices, quit eating meat and drinking alcohol. While he was in the third year of the medical school, he took a break for one full year. During this period he tried the regimen of vegetarian diet and yogic exercises with a group of heart disease patients for one month. The results were very encouraging. He returned to the medical school, completed his studies and received the degree. He again tried his experimental treatment in a much more organised manner. Once again he obtained very good results. He then completed his post-graduation in cardiology, and founded an independent institute. There he conducted with scientific rigour, a clinical trial of his treatment method on heart disease patients and showed that this treatment brings not only a symptomatic relief, but also effectively reduces the blockage in coronaries and opens them up. A real reversal of the coronary heart disease. A scientific paper based on this study was published by *Lancet*, a leading medical journal in the U.K., which gave worldwide publicity to Ornish's method of treating heart disease.

I came across Ornish at the right time in my life. I found his book convincing and liked it. He showed me the way to treat myself, he provided me a definite regimen to follow and gave me hope. I was eager to live and the Ornish method offered a chance. A dying man is desperate to try anything. I decided to stake my life on this gamble.

2.2

On May 13, the fourth day after my angioplasty, I finished reading Ornish's book. I sat up in my hospital bed and asked my sister-in-law to give me paper and pen. Right there and then I wrote down some goals for the next one year --

1. Reduce weight from 72 kg to 65 kg.
2. Eliminate milk and ghee from my diet and make other dietary changes.
3. Reduce the daily food intake to less than 2400 calories.
4. Bring the blood cholesterol level below 150.
5. Bring the blood sugar level below 120 mg on empty stomach and below 180 mg post meal.
6. Exercise every day for half an hour and practise yogic postures for fifteen minutes.
7. Learn '*shavasana*', '*pranayama*' and '*dhyana*' and practise these every day.
8. Get in touch with my own feelings. Get rid of mental stress and re-establish the happy state of mind.
9. Learn music.
10. Search for the spiritual meaning of my life.
11. Bring about a change in the mental attitude. Try to turn my work into '*karmayoga*', i.e. an action from which all expectations of benefit to oneself are effortlessly excluded.

12. Study scriptures like the *Bhagavad Gita*, the Upanishads and devotional literature composed by various saint-poets.
13. Keep coronaries open. I should not suffer angina again and should be able to reach the fourth stage of treadmill test effortlessly.

I have been trying out the Ornish treatment for the past three years. How? What exactly did I do? What were the results? That is what I intend to narrate now.

I did not accept any one Guru. I explored many paths, adopted only that which I found convincing and tried it out on myself. When confused, I sought counsel and guidance from the seniors well known for their personal advancement in spirituality. So, whatever I have tried is a collage of many paths. My search was aided by many people. But I went on making a mental note of everything.

A major credit for my ability to complete these experiments on myself goes to two persons -- Dr. Bidwai and Rani. Dr. Bidwai always welcomed my unconventional experimental approaches with an open mind and encouraged me in my endeavours. Since this treatment implies a complete change in lifestyle, it would have been impossible without the help and active cooperation from Rani. She firmly declined every invitation she received from outside of Gadchiroli or from abroad during the first year of my treatment; and made all the arrangements at home that were necessary for my treatment, took every care of me. She used to say, "I will not debate the worth of whatever you are trying to do, but I will do everything possible in this world to ensure that your health improves and that you remain free from any danger!"

As I write my eyes are filled with tears. During the entire period of my illness, she broke down only once. She was waiting anxiously outside the angioplasty room; on learning that there was a crisis because my coronary artery was torn, she could no longer control herself. She sobbed and wept and said repeatedly in a subdued voice, "This should not have happened to Abhay". Had she not broken down even during this crisis, she would not be human!

My entire effort was, on the one hand, a struggle to stay alive. On the other hand, it was a journey back to the monastic lifestyle in Gandhiji's ashram in Sevagam where my life had begun. The 'healthy lifestyle' recommended by Ornish was, to a large extent, similar to the lifestyle in Gandhiji's ashram.

The result obtained on me is based on an experiment with the sample size of one patient. It cannot be deemed as 'scientific evidence'. Nor do I make such a claim. Ornish has provided the necessary scientifically valid evidence. My intent is to share with others one patient's subjective experience of following this treatment. Though I began to try it out as a treatment of my heart disease, it did not remain limited to the 'treatment' only. It went much beyond. And the exploration has not stopped even now. Something new is happening every day. So I shall narrate my story until now.

2.3

Where shall I begin? Let me begin from where I started and continue in the same order in which I travelled.

After I returned from Lucknow, I stayed at my parent's home near Wardha, a small district town 75 km from Nagpur. My parents, in their 70s, were senior Gandhians, a living example of simplicity, austerity, service and spirituality in action that was the best place for me to recover. I could meet many of my kindred and childhood friends to my heart's content. It also gave me an opportunity to visit two most sacred places in my life -- Vinoba Bhave's ashram in Pavnar and Gandhiji's ashram in a small village, Sevagram – both in Wardha district.

I went to Gandhiji's ashram in Sevagram where my childhood was spent. My early education was completed there. I had known every tree there as my playmate. I had spent time in every hut in that ashram. I visited them all and felt as if I was meeting my long-lost relatives and friends. Finally I entered *'Bapu-kuti'*, the hut in which

Gandhiji used to live[6]. I was familiar with every inch of that austere and sacred dwelling made of wood, bamboo and mud. I felt I had truly returned home! I quietly sat down for a while in Bapu's sitting room. I could intensely feel his presence; I could see him sitting down cross-legged and writing something. I could envision him turning the spinning wheel and drawing a long, continuous thread. After a while, I quietly got up and without disturbing him, came out of his room to sit in the veranda. I saw the trees around *'Bapu-kuti'*. Many of them had been mere saplings when I was a child and had grown along with me for the past 30 or 35 years. They were swaying in the breeze; speaking to me; inviting me.

The day I was admitted to the hospital with a heart attack and anxiously awaited my fate, in those moments of fear and anxiety, Rani had asked me what my last wish would be in case something terrible happened to me. I had answered, "If I die, bury my ashes and bones under some tree near *Bapu-kuti*".

Today, I had returned to *Bapu-kuti* alive. But no matter when I die, my last wish will still be the same. If and when that happens, I will be one with the trees in this ashram. Remains of my body, in the minute form will exist in these trees. Perhaps I will be in the leaves or in the flowers or even in the trunks of these trees; I will be everywhere in these trees. Right here, near *Bapu-kuti*, I will sway in the breeze for hundreds of years. I will breathe here; I will bloom here...sitting in the veranda of *Bapu-kuti* I experienced it all. I was in a deep emotional state; almost like a trance.

I asked Bapu, "Bapu, where did I go wrong?"

I received the answer -- "You will be alright, once again be perfectly healthy."

"What should I do from now on?" -- I asked.

The answer came, "Rid yourself of all desires and hand yourself over to God."

---

6. *Bapu -- literally, 'father'. Ashram inmates and people referred to Gandhji as Bapu. 'Kuti' means hut.*

I stopped asking questions and continued to experience the joy of Bapu's answers.

What was this dialogue that I had engaged in? Was it my own 'inner voice'? Or an illusion generated due to an intense wish? Whatever it was, I received an assurance and a solution.

2.4

My first goal was to make changes in the diet and to thereby reduce my weight and the abdominal girth. When I was a student, I weighed 58 kg. My weight shot up to 70 kg within the first three years of getting married. Then it slowly increased to 73 kg and stayed there for the next 15 years. I wanted to reduce my weight to 65 kg. It became my mental hobby to look at the belly of every person I saw and to contemplate whether he/she will develop 'Syndrome X'. I began to notice that the girth of majority of the men over 30 years of age was on the increase and they were developing a paunch.

We were at the New Delhi airport on our way back from Lucknow. I was fully engrossed in my new hobby of observing the belly of every passenger. Suddenly my attention was drawn to a passenger waiting to board the flight to Jaipur. He seemed to be about 50 years old, but his belly and waist were narrow like a young girl of 15! My eyes riveted on him as if I was watching a great wonder. I drew the attention of Rani and my sister-in-law Padmaja to his slim belly. They started laughing at my silliness.

I said, "Just watch what I do now!" I left the line we were standing in and approached him. I congratulated him on his excellent figure and the slim waist. He was genuinely surprised and looked at me suspiciously. Once he was convinced that I was not making fun of him and that my congratulations were sincere, he relaxed and began to chat with me with great enthusiasm. ("That is better. The goal number eight, open your heart to others". I said to myself!) He was an officer in a bank. He opened up his personal secrets to me -- his slim waist, his work, his family and his family problems. From a distance, I noticed that Rani and Padmaja were having a belly laughter by my 'ludicrous' behaviour, but I did not mind it at all. Like Arjuna's sight transfixed on a bird's eye, I noticed only one thing -- the girth of the belly!

The abdominal girth has now become a very important issue. All the other components of 'Syndrome X' -- high blood pressure, resistance to insulin, increased blood sugar, high blood cholesterol and even heart disease – occur inside one's body; they are invisible from outside. But a large girth (central obesity) is a sign that can be discerned from outside, it can also be measured easily, even at your home. A narrow 'waist like that of a lion' was described in Sanskrit literature as a mark of physical beauty and physical fitness. Science is now confirming the wisdom of that aesthetic norm. So how wide should one's waist be?

Find out the ratio of the girth of the waist to the girth at the level of hips (waist-hip ratio). The circumference of the waist is to be measured midway between the lower ribs and the pelvic crest; the circumference of the hips is to be measured at the widest point. If this waist-hip ratio is 0.85 or better less than 0.80, one is safer. Now, women's hips are naturally wide and, therefore, they can attain the waist-hip ratio below 0.85 relatively easily. However, as soon as the paunch begins to bulge out, men have a hard time maintaining the waist-hip ratio below 0.85. They enter the unsafe zone (ratio larger than 0.85) relatively quickly. As the waistline increases, their lifeline decreases.

My waist-hip ratio was 0.92; it was in the danger zone. In order to reduce both the weight and the waist-hip ratio, I went on the diet recommended by Ornish. As a first step, I drastically reduced the fats in my diet.

On May 13, while I was still in the hospital in Lucknow, I made the decision and from that moment I stopped consuming full fat milk, my most staple diet. Earlier, I used to drink almost a litre of milk every day. I would often drink milk directly from the milk vessel. After we got married, Rani was amazed to see me drink milk in that manner in the kitchen. When I announced from my hospital bed in Lucknow my decision to stop drinking milk, my sister-in-law could not believe that I could ever quit this long standing passion. But the disengagement from the habit occurred almost effortlessly. When needed I began to use the skimmed milk made from the skimmed milk powder. It has zero fats and zero cholesterol. Now I use skimmed milk for whitening my cup of tea or for preparing yoghurt. My skimmed milk consumption is low, at nearly 300 ml each day, thereby my intake of cholesterol and calories from milk has reduced dramatically. I also stopped consuming sugar, ghee, sweets and drastically reduced the intake of any fried foods and ice cream.

According to the Ornish guidelines, I was required to consume no more than 20 grams of oil in a day, and even that was to be non-hydrogenated oil. So the natural question was, "Which oil to be used"? There are three kinds of fats. Saturated fats are abundant in animal fats -- meat, eggs, milk, butter and ghee. Fats that freeze quickly and turn solid (ghee, coconut oil, vegetable oil) are also saturated fats. These are especially harmful to heart, because they cause an increase in blood cholesterol. The other two kinds of fats – mono-unsaturated and poly-unsaturated -- do not increase blood cholesterol. These should be included in the diet, but no oil is good for the heart and one should limit their use.

Ornish recommended using Canola oil, but it is usually not available in India. After studying the analyses of cooking oils generally used in India (Chapter 7, page 185), I concluded that it is best to use an equal mixture of peanut oil, soya bean oil and mustard oil/rapeseed oil for cooking. Those who already have heart disease or those who wish to control their blood cholesterol level should use such a mixture of oils in limited amounts, not more than four teaspoons (20 grams) a day, whether it is used for seasoning the vegetable dishes, spreading on bread, for frying any snacks or consumed in the form of pickles and preserves. And meat, eggs, fish, fried foods and sweets made from the milk products are of course a no-no!

Claims that safflower oil is protective for the heart are lies. Safflower oil is rich in poly-unsaturated fatty acids. Earlier, the poly-unsaturated fatty acids used to be considered as 'protective to the heart'. Later on it was discovered that there are two kinds of poly-unsaturated fatty acids -- Omega-6 and Omega-3. Excessive consumption of 'Omega-6' fatty acids leads to heart diseases as well to cancer. 'Omega-3' fatty acids are good for the heart. The safflower oil is rich in 'Omega-6' type of fatty acids, while mustard oil is rich in 'Omega-3' type of fatty acids. Hence, the mustard or rapeseed oil should be used within the limits mentioned above[7].

My mother often rues that I quit eating ghee and anything containing ghee. Women yearn to feed their loved ones the best food they can cook. But they find it hard to reconcile the traditional perceptions of 'good' and 'bad' dishes with the recommendations of medical science.

Our childhood neighbour, Sulabhavahini, who is now in her early 60s, is very fond of Rani. Since I had to quit consuming my favourite sweets, ghee, milk etc. Sulabhavahini felt very sorry for me. She consoled me, "Abhay, in childhood we desire so many things that we cannot get. As we grow up and are able to afford them, we are no longer able to enjoy them. In our house, we did not have a lot of mattresses. When we had guests staying overnight, the guests were given the mattresses to sleep on and I had to sleep on bare floor. At such times, I used to think that when our finances improve, we shall sleep on plump, soft and comfortable mattresses. Now we can afford those expensive mattresses, but I have a problem with my spinal discs. The doctor advised me to sleep on a hard, stiff bed! And there goes my dream forever!"

---

7. *Dietary theories and recommendations hugely differ. Other 'recommended' diets range from high protein diet, low carb diet to liberal fat diet. Here I am describing Dean Ornish's recommended diet in the 90s that I followed.*

2.5

The need for including 'fibre' in the diet is often mentioned in the literature on healthy diets. Calories and proteins are not the only factors of significance. The Indian National Institute of Nutrition recommends that a daily diet should include at least 40 grams of fibre. Dietary fibres are of two types:

1. **Fibres that do not dissolve** – These are found mainly in the wheat husk. These soften the stools and eliminate the problem of constipation. Once the wheat flour is sifted, the fibres are lost and the remaining flour (called 'maida' in India) contains no fibres. So the soft, white bread made from 'maida' is bad and the brown bread made from flour containing the wheat husk is good for health.

2. **Fibres that dissolve** – These fibres reduce the blood cholesterol and also slow down the absorption of sugar from intestine, thereby preventing the steep rise in blood sugar immediately after a meal. These fibres are found mainly in unpolished rice, whole lentils and beans and, to a lesser extent in carrots, sweet potatoes, potatoes and vegetables. Seeds of fenugreek are abundant in these fibres.

Nutrition science tell us that eating foods devoid of fibre -- bakery products made from 'maida', sugar, milk and fats, sweets, meat and so forth -- meant stressing the body with unnatural diets and inviting a 'disease of modern culture'. (Also see Chapter 7, page 196).

So, now I had to quit eating practically every kind of food that I liked. Or, in fact, I had cultivated a taste for precisely those foods that were actually worth avoiding! I had indulged my taste buds enough. Now the time had come to change both the habit and the liking.

I increased the proportion of fibre rich items, leafy vegetables, spinach, sprouted lentils and fruits in my diet. I started swallowing the four spoonfuls of powdered fenugreek seeds. The abundance of fibre in fenugreek seeds helps reduce the blood sugar as well as cholesterol – my two enemies.

One argument that the proponents of 'nature cure' or 'vegetarianism' often advance considerably appealed to me. It takes thousands of years for the evolution to bring about biological changes in a human body. No significant evolutionary change has occurred in the body of human beings during the last 10,000 years. Our body is no different than that of the earliest human being. Over the thousands of years, the human race has gradually passed through such stages as hunter-gatherers, cattle herders and farmers. However, rapid industrialisation over the past hundred years or so has most radically altered our lifestyle as well as our diet. While we live in a body of the early humans, we want our lifestyle to keep pace with modern times. This is a very strange and unmatched combination indeed! If you attach the body of bus to an aircraft engine and try to make the vehicle run at the speed of an aircraft, surely the body of the bus will break down.

Who is our ancestor? Three million years old bones of a human female were discovered in the vicinity of Lake Victoria in Ethiopia. According to the scientists, this female is the oldest human being whose remains have been discovered to date, so in a way, she is our oldest ancestor. They gave her a name – Lucy[8]. The DNA analysis of a large number of people in various parts of the world shows that nearly 97% of our genes are the same as those of Lucy. Our roots are in the body of Lucy!

I began to think about what Lucy might have eaten. Her body was made to subsist on what kind of food? There was no agriculture in her days. So one can rule out wheat, rice, lentils and oil seeds. Salt, sugar and pepper were unknown. There were no cattle ranches, so there was no milk and no ghee. No one had good weapons, so hunting for meat was not easy either. What then did our great, great grandmother Lucy eat?

Her diet may have been very much like that of the apes, chimpanzees and gorillas. Lucy probably ate everything edible that

---

8. *As new discoveries are made by archaeologists, remains of even earlier human beings continue to come to light.*

could be obtained from the naturally growing plants in her habitat -- leaves, roots and fruits. Her diet contained lots of fibre. Has anyone ever seen monkeys and cows, that live on such a natural diet, suffer from constipation? Biologically, the body of modern man is still designed for the same kind of 'natural' diet, and will remain so for the thousands of years to come. So the question is, how do we bring our diet more or less in line with Lucy's diet?

In Shodhgram, we sponsored contests for preparing meals as close to Lucy's diet as possible. Many people took part in these contests. They used to do the shopping on Sundays. On Mondays they let their imagination loose and cooked very innovative dishes from leafy vegetables, salads, chutneys and soups. Once we had a contest of making milkless *kheer,* porridge like sweet dish usually made from milk, sugar and rice. How could it be prepared without milk? I saw so many varieties of *kheer* made from vegetables that I was amazed by the innovativeness of the contestants.

My reading introduced me to antioxidants. During various chemical metabolic processes in our body, free oxygen radicals are released. These negatively charged oxygen radicals combine with the LDL portion of cholesterol and help the formation of atheromas, the obstructions in blood vessels. Free oxygen radicals can also cause cancer. They play an important role in the genesis of these diseases and in aging of the body. When foodstuffs are fried in boiling oil, these free radicals are formed. However, there are certain ingredients that counter the action of free radicals and protect the body from damage. Such ingredients are called 'antioxidants'. Antioxidants have now become an active field of research and a beacon of hope. The findings to date indicate that fruits, green vegetables, and vitamin E, vitamin C and beta-carotene (vitamin A) act as antioxidants. So, in a way, modern science is leading us to the same kind of vegetables / fruits based natural diet! Lucy's hidden presence in every cell of our body is still ruling supreme even after a million years!

2.6

I discovered three more tricks to improve my eating habits.

It is important to reduce the caloric intake to reduce weight, but without starving oneself. I therefore began to start my meal with vegetable soup, salad, fruits, cucumber, carrot and so forth. I began to insist in our home that only these low-calorie, vegetable dishes be served first and the main course, such as chapati, bread, rice etc. be served later. The 'highly protective' low-calorie items were therefore eaten first, leaving less room in the stomach for other calorie-providing items. My caloric intake thus automatically diminished, but I did not leave the dinner table feeling hungry.

People toil all day so that they can put a decent meal on the table. But what do they do when it is time to eat the meal? They stuff themselves up, paying far less attention to the food and instead chat, watch TV or read a newspaper. Americans go even further and schedule a lunch seminar or a lunch meeting -- a 'working lunch'. The main thing is the meeting, seminar or a work session; meal is only a nuisance!

Once I had attended a retreat on '*vipashyana*' – a Buddhist form of meditation. Since the rule at this retreat was to observe complete silence for 24 hours on all the ten days of the camp, one opened one's mouth only for eating. That made me more attentive to my meal. Just to see what happens, I closed my eyes at the mealtime. Now my attention was totally focused on the food in my mouth. This experience of paying complete attention to eating was new to me. It felt as if the food was bursting with a thousand flavours! My tongue could discern and relish the different flavour of every morsel, of every bit of every morsel. One bite had a 'hard' texture, another one was softer, one was sweet, another one was salty or spicy. It seemed as if my faculty of tasting the smell, the flavour and the texture of food had increased thousand folds. That is what I would call '*bhojan-dhyana*', i.e. meal-meditation. It was the simple every-day food, but the satisfaction I derived from it became far more intense. Besides, it checked any tendency of unnecessary overeating.

What should one do when one is in the company of others who are eating sweets or ice cream or if one gets a sudden urge to eat something sweet? Ornish has suggested one 'trick'. Take a spoonful of your favourite sweet, say ice cream. First look at it very attentively. Observe its colour, smell its aroma, notice its texture and enjoy its splendour. Then, simply place that spoon in your mouth and let it stay there for a while. Let ice cream slowly dissolve in your mouth; the slower, the better. But stop after just one spoonful! In fact, when you eat your most favourite dish, you enjoy only the very first bite and the last bite; rest everything in between is simply gulped down. Therefore, you can get the satisfaction of eating a complete cup of ice cream with just one or two spoonfuls.

I found that Gandhiji had proposed a different idea in his book *'Mangal Prabhat'* (literally, An Auspicious Morning). For those who wish their eating to be determined by the needs to sustain the body and to avoid indulging the taste buds, Gandhiji recommended the regimen of *A-swad*, i.e. Non-taste – (also see Chapter 7, page 195). His proposal was not to eat 'for the taste of it'. How is it that this tongue, this mere four-inch long piece of flesh, makes us dance to its dictates? The tongue is like a litmus paper. Its function is to let us know the taste of the food we place in our mouth. We must not hand over the authority to decide what we should or should not eat to this litmus paper!

2.7

I had aimed to bring my weight down to 65 kg by December of 1995. But meanwhile, I came across the latest report published by the World Health Organisation (WHO). It made me realise that I had been ill informed about the 'normal weight', just as I had been ill informed about the 'normal cholesterol level'. This latest WHO report informed that what had been considered 'normal weight' thus far also fell in the danger zone of the scale. An ideal weight is not to be judged in terms of kilograms alone. It has also to be judged according to a person's height. So, a parameter called 'Body Mass Index' has been proposed as an indicator of normality.

$$\textbf{Body Mass Index} = \frac{\text{Weight in kilograms}}{(\text{Height in meters})^2}$$

Up until now, a body mass index of 25 for men and 28 for women was considered 'normal'. For last 20 years my weight hovered around 73 kg, so my body mass index was 24 and yet I had suffered a heart attack. The new WHO report recommended that the body mass index should be maintained below 22 in order to prevent diabetes and heart disease. It meant that I had to reduce my weight to 62 kg, and not 65 kg. I changed my goal accordingly.

The results of a 12-year study based on monitoring of 320,000 men and women over 30 were published only recently in the *New England Journal of Medicine*, the number one American medical journal. The conclusion of this study was -- For every one-point increase in the body mass index over 21, the risk of death from heart disease increases by 10 percent. However, if the index slips below 18, it implies malnutrition. My new goal of reducing the weight to 62 kg would have resulted in a body mass index of 21. Good!

By the end of December 1995, my weight had reduced to 65 kg just as I had originally intended. After a year of following the Ornish system, i.e. by May of 1996, my weight came down to 62 kg and now it has settled around 58 kg. (Body mass index = 19!). "Am I now underweight?" I wondered. And then I came across WHO Technical Group's another recommendation -- "You had your 'ideal' weight at the age of 25; maintain it for the rest of your life!" When I was 25, I was in the thick of residency in internal medicine at a hospital and I weighed 58 kg! Now I had returned exactly to the same weight. This meant that as soon as I eliminated my errant eating habits, nature had brought my weight back to the original 'ideal' level. Nature needed no weighing scale. The natural intelligence of body seems to be very robust and wise.

I never starved myself, never left the dinner table feeling hungry. I only followed the rules about what to eat and what not to eat. Ornish's advice is, “It does not matter *how much* you eat. What matters is *what* you eat.” ‘*Eat more and weigh less*’ is the title of one of his books. I found that it was really so.

On seeing me a year or so after my angioplasty, Dr. Bidwai said, “Abhay, when people comment that you look like you are wasting away, know for sure that you are doing all right!” In our poverty-stricken famished Indian society, a well filled out rotund physique is deemed as a sign of affluence and therefore desirable. When our villagers see me in the new thinner form, they feel sorry for me. They say, “The doctor is in a really bad health since his illness!” Since Rani is an obstetrician and a specialist in women’s health problems, the traditional midwives (*Dai*) in villages surrounding Shodhgram revere her as a ‘super Dai’. Some of their affection towards Rani is also transferred to me. When they come to Shodhgram for further training or when they bring a patient to us, they see my new appearance and immediately rush to console Rani! To them, I must be sick and hence wasting away. “But our lady doctor is in very good health!”, they commend, which is 20 kilos overweight! These midwives do not know how much unhealthy burden I have shed and how light my heart is now that I have reduced my weight by 15 kg!

However, my tailor is upset with me because he has had to alter my trousers so many times. He has no appreciation for the fact that my waist-to-hip ratio has come down from 0.92 to 0.85. “Your trousers are shapeless now,” he laments.

Four years ago, my blood cholesterol level was 244. When I quit eating cream and ghee, it dropped to 220. I wanted to bring it below 150. One year after I started following Ornish plan, it came down to 142. So now I was in the safe zone as far as the total cholesterol was concerned. But along with the reduction in total cholesterol, my HDL, the ‘protective’ cholesterol, also dropped from 34 to 29. I was now concerned about how to increase my HDL level. I knew that every one milligram increase in the HDL level reduced the probability of heart attack by 2 to 3 per cent. I needed to increase my HDL. The medical books recommended only one way -- exercise!

2.8

Changing my diet alone was not enough. There was no question of my quitting alcohol, smoking or tobacco, as I had always stayed away from these. So regular exercise and reduction of mental stress were other necessary components of the Ornish plan that I needed to follow.

The main cause of diabetes in middle aged persons is the lack of exercise which makes body cells non-responsive to insulin. In due course of time it leads to heart disease and Syndrome X. Since these maladies are in fact 'exercise deficiency diseases', exercise is the only logical remedy.

A term 'aerobics' is often found in the books and the TV programmes on health. What is 'aerobics'? I found out that it was related to what I had learned during my first year in the medical school some thirty years ago. When our muscles are at work, they can receive the necessary energy in two different ways. If one begins exercise without warming up the body for it and suddenly plunges into a vigorous exercise mode, the muscles have to contract in the absence of sufficient supply of blood and oxygen. The energy needed under these circumstances is generated in an anaerobic manner and leads to fatigue after only a short period of intense activity. This has no 'training effect' on the body. Exercises or activities that consist of short stints of exercise followed by brief periods of rest generate energy in the anaerobic manner. Bowling or fielding during the game of cricket or short distance running are typical examples of such activities. If, on the other hand, one prepares the body by way of low intensity warm-up activities and then proceeds to a sustained exercise involving the rhythmic contraction and relaxation of muscles, the energy is generated in the aerobic manner. The warm-up exercise at the beginning permits sufficient time for a proper supply of blood and oxygen to reach the muscles, so that one can exercise for a much longer period of time without experiencing fatigue.

By doing regular aerobic exercise involving large muscles (e.g. walking, running, cycling and swimming), the body derives the benefit of a 'training effect'. It improves the aerobic fitness as well as the fitness of the heart.

"What form of exercise should I choose?" I started thinking. I had not been able to play sports on a regular basis. I had read in Ornish's book that those who walk regularly at a brisk pace for thirty minutes or so, receive the necessary exercise as well as reduce their risk of heart disease by half. 'Exercise' does not necessarily imply becoming a sportsman or a wrestler. A medium intensity exercise is sufficient for reducing the risk of heart disease. It can be accomplished by way of brisk walking for thirty minutes or something equivalent to it on a regular basis.

It comforted me to know that high intensity exercises such as jogging till one is out of breath, weight lifting and sit-ups or push-ups were not necessary. It was also very reassuring to learn that the fitness experts no longer believed in the "no pain, no gain" mantra. An exercise that causes aches and pain is no longer considered necessary for maintaining or achieving physical fitness. On the contrary that false notion of 'no pain, no gain' scares people and turns them away from exercise. I was not aiming to become a body builder or an athlete. I did not have to stretch my body to the point of pain. If an exercise had to be painful, my resolve to exercise regularly would not last. I wanted exercises to be a joyful experience. Medium intensity exercises or sports are joyful.

In the preface to Casey Meyer's book "*Walking*", Dr. George Sheehan writes:

> *In the first book totally devoted to exercise, published in 1955, Christobol Mendez writes: The best and most beneficial exercise is walking. "Mendez gives many reasons for selecting walking. It fulfils all the requirements and is so easy, that no matter where you are, you can do it. Even more important, according to Mendez, walking offers many pleasures and joys.*

He points out that you can observe, read, converse, sing, meditate and practise all your mental skills like imagination, cogitation and memory.

Harry Andrews, the most highly respected track coach at the turn of the century, was another proponent of walking. Andrews included among his athletes Walter George, the world's best at the mile, and the incomparable Alfiee Shrubb, who once held all the world records for distance from two miles to fifteen miles, and many other runners, boxers and cyclists of the time.

Andrews regarded walking as fundamental to all training. "Experience tells me", he writes, "that walking should represent the groundwork for any system of training." It did not matter to him what sport you were in, whether running, boxing, fencing, cycling or rowing; walking as a primary exercise was applicable to all. According to Andrews, "It gave by far the greatest benefit of any form of training in its result."

For those interested only in fitness, walking was his recommended activity. He saw no need to do anything else. It was a superior way to reduce weight and there was no need to worry about pace. "The best advice I can give," he wrote, "is to make your own pace – the pace, in fact, that will suit you best. This pace will almost certainly be an average of four miles an hour."

— *George Sheehan, M.D.*

I chose my exercise. I shall walk every day. After my angioplasty, I had gradually started walking while I was still in the hospital. In June, after returning to Shodhgram, I started going for a walk every day. Whenever I went for a walk, Rani used to recall April 18, the day I suffered from angina, and she used to be extremely anxious until I returned home. Her worrying about me in fact gave me a secret pleasure. In the olden days, when a warrior went to the battlefield, his wife used to anxiously pray at home and wait for the husband to return home safely. I got a similar feeling. It was thrilling. Walking indeed was my battle!

How far should one walk? At what pace? How should one walk? What precautions should one take while walking? To address these questions, a new 'science of walking' is evolving.

Walking has been the most persistent activity during the 3 million years of known history of mankind. However, the technique of walking learnt during the early childhood cannot be entirely depended upon. A new science of walking will need to be developed and learnt! It will become a new yoga. I have fondly named it in Sanskrit, '*Char-yoga*' i.e. a yoga of walking.

Starting with half kilometre a day, within two months I progressed to walking three kilometres a day. In July, I took the treadmill test in which I was able to walk fast till my heart rate reached 189 per minute. The target heart rate for my age was 175, so I could reach more than 100% heart rate expected of me. It meant that the angioplasty had completely opened my arteries and that I could safely exercise vigorously.

I increased my pace of walking to one kilometre in ten minutes and walked three km each day. I had managed to walk briskly. Every day, after an initial warm up of about half km, I slowly increased my pace to six km per hour, walked three km at this speed and finally walked another half a kilometre for cooling down. Together, it came to a four-km walk every day. For an average man, both this pace and the distance provide sufficient exercise.

I also found the prescribed way to judge whether the daily exercise was adequate. Subtract your age from 220. The resulting number represents the highest heart rate you should aim at. If you are 50 years old, the maximum (100%) heart rate for you is 170. You should gradually reach up to 80% to 85% of this heart rate over a span of a few weeks by increasing the intensity of your exercise (Chapter 7, page 205). At my age of 45, the maximum heart rate would be 175 (220-45). Moreover, 80% of 175 is 140. So, my regimen was to bring my heart rate to 140 in a 5-minute warm-up, maintain the heart rate at 140 for the next 30 minutes and to finally cool down for 5 minutes, adding up to a 40 minute walk every day.

In the beginning, since I was not used to any exercise at all, my heart would start beating at the rate of 140 per minute as soon as I reached the walking speed of six km per hour. But, as I began to exercise regularly, the brisk walking at the speed of six km per hour was not sufficient to make my heart beat at the rate of 140 per minute. It would not go beyond 125 per minute. This was a sure sign of improvement in the cardiac fitness. But I wanted to exercise which would make my heart beat at the rate of 140 per minute. For that purpose, I found another method -- 'aerobic' walking, a fast walk (Chapter 7, page 203). Aerobic walking pushed my heart rate to 150 and I found that the exercise from such fast-paced walking was as intense as jogging.

At the end of six months, in November 1995, I put myself through the next physical challenge. I started cycling. It brought new worries to Rani. Starting with four kilometres on the first day, I cycled further and further each day. The day I rode ten kilometres, I telephoned my friends and relatives and told them about my 'victory'. Then I added a little bit of jogging to my daily walk. During jogging, I could safely increase my heart rate to 180. As if I was taking a daily treadmill test in the woods of Gadchiroli and proving myself healthy each day.

In fact, this intense exercise was not necessary. I was simply testing myself in order to confirm the healthy state of my heart. Having passed these tests successfully, I felt great relief. "Now I am healthy. Free from heart disease!" The joy of freedom cannot be adequately described.

Must everyone follow the routine of a morning walk? In the U.K., taking children to school in family automobile has become one of the responsibilities of parents. It deprives the children of an opportunity of their daily exercise. So, a new movement began -- "Walk the children safely to school." In India, this would be a very welcome concept for the families who live in cities -- they have gotten into the routine of cramming their children in an auto-rickshaw and sending them off to school. How wonderful would it be, if they walked to school? Sports and sport matches are also excellent forms of exercise for school children. I would like to add, however, that the emphasis should be on their playing; it should not become a competitive activity and add one more stressful burden to the children's life.

A novel idea originated in Ireland -- they put up the signboards along the road announcing how far you have walked. These signboards are very encouraging to those who walk for exercise. The government of the Netherlands went one step further. If people would use bicycles instead of cars, they naturally will get the exercise and the parking problems in cities will be solved. People in the Netherlands started using bicycles on a large scale. But, as a consequence, thefts of parked bicycles became a problem in cities. The cost of engaging a police force to search and find a stolen bicycle was more than the price of a brand new bicycle! The Dutch government took a positive step. One day, they placed 4,000 new bicycles everywhere in Amsterdam and allowed people to use them, take home free of cost! Use of bicycles increased and bicycle thefts stopped completely!

It is not always necessary to seek exercise out of the house. It is not even possible in many large cities. In fact the outdoor exercise is an unproductive activity. Some fifty or sixty years ago, Vinoba Bhave wrote an essay "*Teen Grih-devata*" (Three Household Goddesses). He suggested that the household manual work should be "worshipped" as a form of prayer. "The hand-mill not only grinds grain into flour, but also grinds away the laziness and sickness", he wrote. "What is the use of saving labour? It will not save your life. But our people now dislike physical labour to the extent that they want to save labour even at the cost of life!"

In today's context, I would choose three '*grih-devata*' to be a broom, a hand-mill and a spade. It would entail adequate exercise, useful work output, and, if one puts his or her heart into it, it is almost like meditation. Sweeping the house and the yard with a broom is a light exercise, grinding the flour for the household is a medium level exercise and wielding a spade to dig the soil and to plant trees is a high intensity exercise. One could exercise this way for up to half an hour each day in accordance to one's ability. One could include all three forms of exercise in the half hour routine.

The last word on this subject, though it sounds like a suggestion by Vinoba, is actually a recommendation by the National Institute of Health, US -- "The work (physical labour) that makes you sweat and pant a little is a medium intensity exercise. Everyone should perform such work for at least half an hour a day. The daily household chores are therefore an excellent form of exercise."

Every day, I started going for walk in the woods on that same path to Kudakvahi. Our five dogs invariably accompany me. It is their time to be petted by me, to express their affection and to declare their trust. It is my time to meet the rising sun. Every tree on the path eagerly waits to see me. Had I ever experienced the changing colours, scents and shapes of trees with this intensity earlier? Recently, I read the memoirs of Henry Thoreau. Upon seeing neatly dressed Thoreau walking hurriedly towards the woods, someone asked him where he was headed for. Lost in his own thoughts, Thoreau answered, "I must hurry. I have an appointment with one tree in the woods!" I am hopeful that trees in the woods of Gadchiroli will one day talk to me like that. But, right now, I am happy with the love they shower upon me.

My eyes began to notice the serene beauty of the surroundings during my daily walks. The seasons changed. The forms changed too. I started carrying a camera with me. I captured many shapes and forms of the Palash, Moha and Kumbhi trees on the camera. Some of the shots turned out beautiful pictures. I enlarged those prints and placed them everywhere in Shodhgram. Now one could enjoy the beauty of these flowers all year round.

I found yet another benefit of walking for exercise. You develop a sense of intimacy with your muscles. The muscles begin to talk to you. You feel like you have re-established your relationship with your body.

The instrument of body gets tuned. The body and the mind resonate together. Walk in such a way that the rhythm of your feet matches with the rhythm of your breathing. Breathe in while you walk three steps, breathe out for the next four steps. Your breathing, your feet, your body and your mind become one symphony. Walking becomes like singing a song. At the same time, the nature surrounding you also affects you. Tall trees, the distant clouds and the ever-receding horizon expand your vision. Your vision acquires a new dimension of grandeur. In our routine life, the office door, walls of the commuter train compartment and the bedroom ceiling limit the range of our vision and the horizon shrinks to a distance of fifteen feet. Gradually, the mind also is limited by an expanse of fifteen feet! But when you go out for a walk in open air, the entire forest, the entire sky and the entire sun fill your vision; the horizon expands. And gradually, the mental horizon also expands to include the entire universe -- at least for a few moments.

About two kilometres behind the confines of Shodhgram, a little stream flows through the woods. I started going there. I let the dogs romp around in the water while I sat on a large rock and watched the stream. There was nothing specific to watch as such. No specific intention, either. I just watched that rivulet flow by, the leaves rustle and the rays of sun filter through the leaves. Out there was nature, dancing by its rules, to its own rhythm. Inside my mind too, there was a dance of another nature. The nature out there and the nature inside my mind were parts of one and the same cosmic truth. But, there stood a partition between the two -- a partition of my 'I'-ness. That partition would not allow the two to merge with each other and to dance in the same rhythm. Could this 'I'-ness ever be forgotten? Could it ever be dissolved away? How? How?

*****

3. Being in the Moment

Sitting quietly
Doing nothing
Spring comes and
grass grows
by itself.

— A Zen haiku

3.1

I had turned to yoga because I wanted to live. Ornish had recommended *yogasanas* (yogic postures) and *dhyana* (meditation). During my childhood in Sevagram I had learnt a few *yogasanas,* but I had never practised these regularly. I did not know what exactly was meant by '*yoga*', but I had heard that the practitioners of yoga acquired the ability to control their heart rate. So I was hopeful that by practising yoga, I could restore the health of my heart.

There was no one to teach me yoga in the woods of Gadchiroli. Following the suggestion of my father, I wrote to honourable Ms. Vimalatai Thakar[9] and asked her where and how I could learn yoga. She recommended Dr. Phadnis of Pune and Dr. Gunde of Kolhapur. Both of them offered me excellent guidance. Another well-wisher, Dr. Bharati Amte gave me some books, cassettes and the addresses of some centres of yoga. In a bookstore I came across two excellent books written by Mr. B. K. S. Iyengar -- '*Light on Yoga*'-- a book on *yogasanas* and '*Light on Pranayama*'. With the help of these books and cassettes, I began to learn yoga by myself. A general admonition in this field warns that you should not try to start the practice of yoga and *pranayama* without a guru. You may make grievous errors in the

---

9. *Ms. Vimalatai Thakar is well-known in India as well as in several Western countries as a spiritual teacher. She is a disciple of J. Krishnamurti and well-versed in Hindu scriptures including the Upanishads. She emphasizes the practice of yoga, even by householders, both men and women, in order to make any progress on the path of spirituality. She had walked alongside Vinoba Bhave the length and the breadth of India in order to convince wealthy landowners to donate land to poor peasants. Though her first name is Vimala (the pure one), she is often referred to by everyone as Vimalatai, the elder sister Vimala, as a mark of deep respect for her spirituality and her teachings.*

absence of proper coaching. But I had no other choice. I had to stay in the forest and learn myself like Ekalavya[10].

I selected twenty yogic postures, which I thought were most useful to me and began to practise those every day. The yogic postures toned my muscles and gave me a feeling of a certain control over my own body. I followed my morning walk up with *surya-namaskara* (sun postures – a series of 12 postures), other yogic postures and finally with *shavasana*. *Shvasana* is simply a posture in which one lies motionless on one's back like a '*shava*' or a corpse. Because of the association of this posture with the word '*shava*', I disliked it during my childhood. It never caught my fancy, nor did I ever think of any benefits accruing from it. But, that was my childhood perception. Now my world had turned upside down. It was necessary to learn and to experience everything anew. Who knows, I might find the right path in this!

Since it was a question of my life or my death, I was willing, nay, eager to try everything.

So I began. I used to lie in my own bed and try to attain the posture of *shavasana* while instructing my mind to become still. But I could hear the sounds of pots and pans in the kitchen, I could hear Rani talking to someone, I could hear the noise my children made. Distractions like these would not let me focus my attention on *shavasana*. So I moved to the study in the basement of the house. It provided me necessary privacy and there was lack of distractions.

My own attempts to instruct my mind to become still and to lie motionless like a corpse often resulted in my falling asleep. Sometimes the mind would wander off on its own and the link necessary for *shavasana* would break. On becoming aware of it, I used to get angry with myself. So I started playing the recorded cassette and following the instructions. It prevented my falling asleep and the wanderings

---

10. *Ekalavya -- A character in the great Sanskrit epic 'Mahabharata'. When the royal teacher taught the art of archery to the Pandava and Kaurava princes, Ekalavya, who belonged to the tribe of aborigines, observed it from a distance and then practised by himself. He self-taught and became extremely skilful in archery and surprised all the princes as well as their royal teacher.*

of my mind. After using the cassette for about twenty days, I did not need it any longer. I could play the cassette in my mind.

Shavasana involves relaxing the muscles one by one. As the tension accumulated in each muscle is let out, a stress-free state of ease and comfort is reached. I found out that no matter how much of tension is gotten rid of, the muscles could be relaxed further. I began to wonder how much tension and stress we allow to build up in our limbs! While relaxing the wrinkles between my eyebrows, reducing the pressure inside the eyelids and relaxing the tight muscles of my jaw, I wondered how up till then I had never been aware of how much tension I needlessly carried.

Maintaining the *shavasana* posture for ten to fifteen minutes was an experience of incomparable joy. My entire body felt as if it was born anew. I practised the *shavasana* routinely after yogic postures in the morning. In addition, I practised *shavasana* again after lunch and followed it with a nap for fifteen minutes. That brief nap was far more refreshing than an hour-long sleep! (In America, they arrange a lunch seminar. That means they insist on working even through the lunch! In Italy, Greece and Southern France, there is a custom of an hour-long siesta after the lunch at mid-day. Americans succumb to mental stress and heart diseases, while in Italy, Greece and France the incidence of heart disease is the lowest among all the developed countries).

I also discovered that *shavasana* after lying down in the bed at night helped me fall asleep quickly and led to a very relaxed and restful sleep. "One can even learn to sleep well!" I wondered. "How did I manage to sleep for the first 45 years of my life without acquiring this basic skill?"

I used the cassettes on *shavasana* made by various yoga teachers. They offered many new and useful suggestions. The basic relaxation technique in *shavasana* is with eyes closed, to focus the attention on one part of body at a time, to experience the sensation at that location and to let go it into a relaxed state. Some people have used a beautiful word for this -- *'avayava-dhyana'*. (In Sanskrit, *'avayava'* means an body organ, a part). Indeed, as you focus your attention on each part, not only does that part relax, but the mind also stops wandering around. It is as if the mind meditates on that part of body. *Shavasana* is a mental exercise more than a body posture. It is a body-meditation.

I came across a cassette titled *'Yoga-nidra'* ('*nidra*' means sleep). I liked the technique of *yoga-nidra.* I mail-ordered the cassettes and books on this technique from the Bihar School of Yoga in Munger where this technique was originally developed. *Yoga-nidra* includes positive auto-suggestions in addition to *shavasana*. The logic behind these auto-suggestions is that when one repeats a message in a fully relaxed but alert state, it exerts a deep influence on one's mind. So I made up a message for myself -- "I will practise yoga and *dhyana* and I will become perfectly healthy". Later, I added a few more words -- "I will practise yoga and *dhyana* and I will become perfectly healthy, I will live to be 100 and I will do *nishkama karma*" (duty without desiring a benefit for myself). Later on I followed the method of Stephen Covey to make up my own mission statement and started repeating that statement during the practice of *yoga-nidra.* During *yoga-nidra*, the body is fully relaxed, but the mind is fully alert and receptive. It is like a hypnotic trance. The chanting of your mission statement in such a state of consciousness allows it to penetrate deep in the mind may be to take a root in the unconscious.

I found one step in *yoga-nidra* very useful -- focussing the attention on breathing after one has relaxed the body by means of *'avayava-dhyana'*. Breathe in very slowly, breathe out slowly and keep a count. As the mind is focussed on breathing in and breathing out, it does not wander and this activity itself becomes a *dhyana*.

Both body and mind are 'rejuvenated' by *shavasana* or *yoga-nidra*. I became aware of one more effect. Having dropped the guard and given up the defences, the body lay perfectly still, breathing went on automatically at its own natural pace and the mind remained still. I then began to realise that everything was happening without *me* doing anything. In fact I did not carry my burden. I had a sudden realisation of what Tukaram, one of the greatest poet-saints of Maharashtra, wrote in the 17th century, "God, though I believe that I am walking, you are the one who carries my burden!" This was really true!

I was not breathing, I was not exerting any wilful effort. And yet, everything was happening – smoothly by itself! Someone else was making it happen, someone else was shouldering the responsibility of my life. I was simply an existence. I only experienced my existence. I simply was. And this was a blissful state of being -- an effortless existence, without any exertion, without any sorrow. As Saint Tukaram said, this was indeed "A gentle wave of delight in the lake of blissful joy".

If such a state can last for fifteen minutes, why can't it be experienced all the time? *Shavasana*, by releasing all tensions from body and mind, trains one to experience with equanimity the joy of simply being, simply existing. That indeed is a spiritual experience.

If I were given the power, I will award the Nobel Prize for Medicine and for Peace to the person who developed the technique of *shavasana*. But, that person never took out a patent for it, nor did he attach his own name to this technique. He left no trace of himself. He must be the master of the art of self-effacement, a *'nishkama-karmayogi'* indeed!

3.2

Though I had started regular walks, and yogic postures along with *shavasana,* I also took my medicines regularly. Once in a while I used to be overcome with intense anxiety or the feeling of losing ground. Even for minor chest pains due to other causes or on feeling extremely tired, we had resorted to panic ECG right away during these days. The physician in me would start calculating the probability of another heart attack. When everything seemed to be going right, suddenly, in December of 1995, my heart began to beat irregularly; extra-systoles began to appear in between the regular beat. Both Rani and I were very worried. We called on Dr. Bidwai again. However, once he assured us, I accepted those irregular heartbeats. They visit me now and then even to this day.

As time went on, I realised that I had begun to have a much better communication with my own body. I could listen to the 'song' of my body, its tune and I knew if it was out of tune even slightly. As a physician, I diagnose my patients every day. But I was becoming aware of my own body at a far subtler level. This was not a result of my medical education. This was a natural language, a language without words, which every living animal can understand. Many patients can understand it, if they have not lost their touch with their own selves. Yes, our body does talk to us a lot!

This new understanding helped boost my confidence that if my heart ever became sick again, I would know it. Once my mother heard me talking about my illness. She said, "Please do not talk about such morbid things again in my presence. I cannot bear it." I said, "Mother, I am talking about what happened to me in the past. Now I am not unwell anymore. And if I am to suffer from another heart attack, I will know about it in advance, so you do not worry."

What I said to my mother was not by way of mere consolation to ease her mind. I do feel confident of what I said to her. Now I rely on my inner signals to a much greater extent. And my inner signals are telling me that my heart is alright. At least, that reduced my anxiety and built up a sense of confidence.

Why did I take Ornish so seriously? He did not advise anything new that the ancient Indian science of yoga had not explained already. However, my stubborn faith in modern science had made me close my mind to the traditional medical system. What then brought about this change?

I was in dire need. I desperately wanted to live. I wanted to live a healthy life and I knew the limits of modern medical science, I had a first-hand experience of it. So my mind had become receptive to the idea of trying out other ways.

But why Ornish's method? Why not any other?

First of all, there existed in my mind a hidden attraction towards yoga and *dhyana* since long. One may call it an influence of the Indian traditions. So my mind readily agreed to experiment with it. I would not have been ready to experiment with say the 'magnet therapy'.

Secondly, and unlike other proponents of traditional or alternative therapies, Ornish did not say, "Our scriptures say so" or "Trust, because I say!" He backed up his claims with scientific evidence. His experimental methodology was rigorous, his scientific evidence was irrefutable and hence his claims appealed to me. Braunwald's book on heart diseases and Ornish's research papers spoke the same language of science with equal rigour.

Thirdly, Ornish did not speak only of freedom from bodily illness. I had already experienced how fragile and momentary this body could be. Now I had developed a keen interest in problems that transcended the body. I saw in Ornish's therapy a scope for the fulfilment of the physical, mental and also the spiritual needs.

Besides, the lifestyle that Ornish recommended included vegetarianism; it was a lifestyle that minimised one's needs, a lifestyle that emphasized disciplining both the mind and the body, a lifestyle that brought about a genuine union of people with one another. That lifestyle was in sync with my own social convictions. That is why I took up to Ornish's therapy and the new lifestyle with such enthusiasm and determination.

3.3

Up to this point, it was relatively easy to narrate my efforts and experiences. It was all about the diet, the exercise and the body. But from here on I am going to try narrating my experiences of *dhyana* and my spiritual journey. This is not my forte. This was an unfamiliar path for me. I was often confused, lost my way, doubts repeatedly overwhelmed me, I returned to the same point again and again instead of making any progress; I was often exhausted and frustrated. But I also saw a dim light at a distance. So I kept trying. This was a journey within. I shall narrate it just the way it happened.

I had harboured a curiosity and lurking fascination for spirituality, *dhyana* (meditation), and *samadhi* (a state of wakeful trance) for a long time; but since I was all wound up in the day-today tasks of life and work, I had shelved this agenda as something to be done later. However, Ornish had placed heavy emphasis on *dhyana*. Moreover, now there was nothing like 'later' in my life. Probably that 'later' stage of my life had already arrived! At any rate, I did not want to die just yet; but there was no guarantee as to when the death might strike. I did not wish to die without experiencing what *dhyana* might offer, so I began to seek out the path of *dhyana.*

I started off with *dhyana* as a therapy for my heart disease, but gradually the object of my search changed. "What is the meaning of my life?" "How will I have a revelation of the divine?" "How will I attain what yogis call a state of liberation?" I grew eager to find answers to these questions before death caught up with me. With the hope that *dhyana* will provide me the answers and that I will certainly see the other side of this mundane and banal existence, I redoubled my efforts. I was always aware of the sword that hung over my head.

I began with the practice of *pranayama*[11] and *dhyana* with the help of the cassettes made by a Christian nun named Vandana mata. This involved sitting alone in a quiet place and focussing the attention on the activity of breathing -- breath awareness. As I did that, the instruction in the cassette suggested associating with each inhalation

---

11. *Pranayama -- Breath is considered 'prana' or the life force in the science of yoga. 'Ayama' is simply a technique of regulating. Thus 'Pranayama (prana + ayama)' is the technique of regulating the breath. Ordinarily, breathing is an involuntary activity of the body. But, a practitioner of pranayama can bring the activity of breathing under one's own conscious control.*

and exhalation the feeling "this is what unites me with the universe". My breath was the bridge of union with the universe! That was a wonderful idea, and yet, literally true! The cassette further instructed the repetition of the mantra '*So-Hum*'[12] to let that feeling become well-established in the mind.

I had heard a lot about *vipashyana.* I attended a ten-day retreat in Igatpuri and learnt about two Buddhist methods of meditation -- *anapana* and *vipashyana*[13] along with an introduction to Buddhist ethics. From the Bihar School of Yoga, I learnt the technique of 'empty mind *dhyana'.* Through the books and cassettes I obtained from the USA, I learnt some more techniques of *dhyana* and the technique of 'imagery and visualisation'. I also read what Acharya Rajaneesh has written about various techniques of *dhyana.* The best guide I met was of course Vimalatai Thakar. Not only is her mastery in this field well recognised, but her style of offering guidance with loving care and not demanding anything in return in the form of loyalty or faith appealed to me. I received her guidance through her books and letters as well as through my personal visits to her.

I sat down in a quiet place each morning to practise *dhyana*. The basement of our house became my cave, the special place of learning and for practising *dhyana*. I had in my mind an acute curiosity and a burning thirst for revelation. What it meant I did not know. In fact, I did not know clearly what I expected to happen. Something should happen. That divine principle ought to be revealed to me. This yearning should end!

And talk of the obstacles! Even when my eyes were closed, every noise outside bothered me. If someone yelled in the house, if a pot or a pan crashed to the floor, if a motorcycle passed by... each noise evoked in my mind a reaction, a sense of anger over the

---

12. *So-Hum -- Literally, "That I am". It is an awareness that a disciple should cultivate in his mind after the guru has taught him "That thou art (Tat tvam asi)" a basic tenet of Hindu spiritualism called advait - vedanta.*

13. *Anapana is a method of developing intense breath awareness, and vipashyana, literally meaning a special insight, special vision, is a method of meditating over your body sensations.*

disturbance. After suffering from the disturbances for long, a simple trick suggested by Dr. Phadnis helped. “Change the way you react to these disturbing noises. Do not fret and fume, do not say “what a nuisance!” Simply stop thinking about the noise and listen to it calmly – as if you are listening to the birds calling each other”. In a way, this was like making the noise the object of meditation. Slowly, these noises ceased to bother me.

In the beginning, I was not able to sit in *padmasana* -- the lotus position for my *dhyana.* My legs were too stiff. When I was young, Vinoba Bhave himself had once tried to teach me how to sit in the lotus pose, but I had not been able to. I gave up on the lotus pose. I should at least, be able to assume the earlier *siddhasana* pose. However, when I tried that, one knee would stay floating far above the ground, my legs used to get sore and fatigued; and in five or ten minutes they used to become absolutely numb, forcing me to break out of the pose. In the *vipashyana* camp, one had to sit in a steady pose for an hour at a time, and during a typical day, for ten to twelve hours a day. It was an excruciating torture for me. I used to curse myself, “You cannot even sit in a simple pose; when will you master *dhyana?”*

The daily struggle began to slowly make my legs supple. After three years, I could easily sit in the *siddhasana* pose and maintain it for a long time without pain. I also found that folding up a blanket or bed-sheet into a narrow, three-inch thick roll and resting the base of the spine on it while sitting made it easier to assume the *siddhasana* pose. As a matter of fact, Iyengar’s book does mention this suggestion. But it took me a long time to actually try it out and to recognise its importance. Indeed, mere availability of guidance is not enough. To accept it, you should feel the need for it deep within you. You have to open the doors of your mind and let that teaching enter. Then you need practice to internalise that teaching. It took me three years to overcome the simple problem of how to sit!

I began the practice of *pranayama.* To read books, experiment, experience whatever happens and move ahead – that was my way, a path of stubbed toes and hurtful woes. I focussed my attention on inhaling and exhaling to feel and see it as a medium of uniting with the nature or with the divine principle. The incoming breath is called *'puraka'* (the 'filler') in the yogic terminology. It came from the nature outside and I began to see that it brought with it the gift of life. I accepted it as if it were a blessing from Him and consciously carried it deep inside my chest. When I exhaled, I envisioned I was letting go my ego, the one that cried out for self-identity, and an incorrigible separateness from the rest of the universe. It facilitated, exhalation by exhalation, envisioning a state of union with the nature, a state of total dissolution of the self in the nature. In fact, the cycle of inhalation and exhalation is continuously going on, all 24 hours, by itself. I was only assigning a new meaning to it. Was this practice of *pranayama* really a conscious effort to assign the process of breathing a new meaning? "Assigning?" I wondered. "Or, whether that meaning has always been there, only it is now that I am learning to experience it?"

Swift movements of the mind, the mind running helter-skelter during the practice of *dhyana* is an amazing thing. You secure a quiet place and sit down in the *siddhasana* pose, you close your eyes and you train your attention of the incoming and the outgoing breath. But does the mind sit still? No! Is it like a gust of wind or is it like a drop of mercury? No matter what you do, you cannot catch it with your fingers; you just cannot hold it in your fist.

You start the *dhyana* practice. For a few moments, you experience a silence, a silence devoid of any thoughts. You feel good. You say to yourself, "Wow! I have got it! For the past so many seconds, there have been no thoughts coursing through the mind!" And suddenly you realise that this too is a thought; your mind has not been quiet and still after all! What you have had was only an illusion of a quiet, empty mind!

Then you give up on the idea of emptying your mind of all thoughts. You decide to simply observe its movements without getting involved or trapped in its games. For a few moments, everything is quiet, the mind is still. And then a thought peeps in like an innocent little squirrel -- "The hospital inventory of medicines is down. Will have to order more from Nagpur." The thought pops up, but I simply look at it and it disappears. Another one pops up -- "The *palash*[14] tree was in full bloom today. Looked so marvellous! How apt is its English name -- Flame of the Forest!" I keep looking at this thought also and it too disappears. Suddenly I feel as if an ant is creeping up my left thigh. My mind speaks up -- "What could this be? An ant? Would it bite me? Oh no! When one is practising *dhyana*, such illusions will surely arise. I should not be taken in by it. When the Buddha sat down for his penance, what fantastic and fearsome illusions tried to distract him! But hey! I am no Buddha...." But I have not moved my thigh even a little bit and that sensation of the ant creeping up the thigh is gone. Another thought enters -- "See! If you do not let your mind be distracted by these thoughts, you do succeed! That sensation of an ant vanished by itself! Yes, you are surely progressing in the practice of *dhyana*! You did it! You chased the ant away! You have succeeded!"

Thus starts the play of mind.

During the course of my reading, I came across several techniques of *dhyana.* There was something useful in each technique and it made me feel fresh and good after I tried it out. But as I read more and tried out many things, I became quite confused as to which one of these techniques and rites was the most appropriate for me. I wanted to practise *dhyana* and become very adept at it, but there were so many ways to get there. Which path should I follow? I did not have much time left. Even that was getting shorter as each day passed by. I may miss my bus. I felt deep anguish. "Which path should I follow? Which method will lead me to the revelation? Please help!"

The days passed by. My practice of *dhyana* was accompanied by daily reading, yogic postures and *pranayama*. They started getting interconnected. As I progressed on all four fronts, I was visited by new experiences such as sudden burst of very pleasant tingling all over body, spells of uncontrollable euphoria or fleeting moments

---

14. *Palash -- Name of a deciduous tree native to the wooded areas in India. In March, new leaves sprout and by April its bright red and orange flowers are in full bloom.*

of awareness that I had 'sensed' something totally different while looking at something quite ordinary and familiar. Once I experienced a state of a soundless, peaceful void, the mind keenly awake yet completely void of any thoughts. This experience was like floating on a sea of happiness and it lasted for nearly forty or fifty minutes! My mind eagerly asked, "What is this? Is this what they mean by *dhyana?* Is this what they mean when they talk about 'the experience of a blissful state'? I tried several times to recapture that blissful state, but it eluded me.

Books on *dhyana* had cautioned the seeker against such momentary and elusive experiences. These are nothing more than a passing scenes on the way. One should not become infatuated by these. It is likely that such illusions of bliss are spawned by the heightened sensitivity of the mind or by the intense anticipation. My psychiatrist friend Dr. Anand Nadkarni, called it 'a trance'. Vinoba calls such experiences *'pratibh darshan'.* It is not 'the vision', but only an assurance that you are progressing on the right track. However, one ought not to remain in its thrall; one is better off leaving these alone and moving on. You cannot relive those transient moments of rapture, one cannot bring them by force. When I understood this, the lingering temptation of such experiences fell away.

During the course of my journey, questions sometimes used to cloud my mind and doubt plagued the faith. But then, the answer used to present itself from somewhere around. Perhaps these answers were always there; only the questions had never occurred to me before. When the need and the curiosity forced me to look for them, the right answers seemed to appear at the right time. An answer was found sometimes in what I was reading, sometimes in someone else's experiences, sometimes in a simple sentence or a phrase somebody uttered, sometimes in someone's teachings and sometimes in nature. When intense questions arose and the mind longed for answers, the answers arrived.

Things began to fall in place one after the other. I read some books by Vimalatai. Her booklet '*Meditation in Daily Life*' is a gift to those who wish to make progress in the practice of *dhyana.* *'Mahaguhame Pravesh'* (*In the deep cave*) by Vinoba came across to me as a priceless book. It dispelled many illusions and fanciful notions about *dhyana* I had accumulated. *Dhyana* is not the practice of a specific technique, nor the following of a specific path. It is a state of consciousness wherein you fully experience the essence of your existence beyond words and beyond thoughts. It is futile and meaningless to draw up a timetable for attaining such a state. You can only cleanse your mind and wait for that event. Uninvited and unannounced, without forced efforts, that state is suddenly yours to experience. You cannot make it happen or make it happen a moment sooner by trying hard. You need to plough the soil and wait for the rains. You cannot make the rain.

This much became clear to my intellect. I had not had the revelation or the grand experience. The rains had not arrived yet. I was still only in the process of yoking the oxen to a plough. But the acceptance of this fact lightened the burden of expectations and anticipations. The confusion grew thinner. I once again approached the daily practice of *dhyana* with renewed enthusiasm. On several occasions, my attention became focussed with little effort. But, there is no guarantee of your mind. Some days it behaved like a stubborn mule and no matter what I tried, my mind would not cooperate. On a day like that, there was nothing else to do but to accept it and let go of the practice.

3.4

When I was still a student, I had read *My Experiments with Truth*, the autobiography of Gandhiji. A lot of water had flown under the bridge since then. I felt I should read it again. "May be, his experiences will guide me," I hoped. I came across many useful things in his autobiography.

In his biography by Louis Fischer I came across Gandhiji's one statement that made the deepest impression. In his meeting with Nobel Prize winner and French writer Romain Rolland, Gandhiji said, "God is not a person, God is an eternal principle." In my earlier readings this statement had completely escaped my attention. I had no definite opinion about God's existence or non-existence. The word God, evoked an image of a crowned, radiant man seated on a heavenly throne, etched in my childhood memories by mythological stories and ubiquitous pictures. Though the intellect and the reason would not permit a belief in the existence of such God, I was never able to firmly deny God's existence either. So God remained an unresolved dilemma. But when this time I read Gandhiji's statement, I suddenly felt that if God is not some shining eminence sitting on a heavenly throne, but if God is a principle, He may really exist. But if God is a principle, then what principle? And in what form?

Further, Gandhiji says, "Truth is God!" I felt this statement was exceptionally bold and experiential. All faiths proclaim that God is true, but Gandhiji asserted, "Truth itself is God!" If Truth is God, then verily, God must exist, because there is no doubt that truth exists. In fact, by definition, whatever exists is, 'the truth'. Does it mean 'Whatever is, is God?'

It was a lightening revelation! Gone was the doubt about God's existence that my scientific training had planted in my mind. Gandhiji had turned the traditional equation "God = Truth!" around and proclaimed "Truth = God!" Mathematically, it was absolutely correct, and, with that proclamation, all my doubts and confusions cleared as if a beam of bright light had suddenly been flashed. Indeed, if Truth were God, then God could be searched, could be sought, could be seen, God would be revealed, God could be experienced!

In his commentary on *Ishavasya Upanishad,* Vinoba has provided a penetrating insight into the unity of Truth and God. At one place he says,

"Is God the Truth or is Truth the God?
One is a language of philosophers, the other is the language of the seeker."

Even if both mean one and the same, the point of view "Truth is God" is more useful for the aspirants of spirituality. One can always begin with the search for Truth because it is more tangible, with form. Since God is formless, intangible and transcends any description, one cannot begin with the search for God.

Gandhiji had said, "God is a principle." What did he mean? In Sanskrit, the word for 'a principle' is *tattva* (*tat* + *tva*). '*Tat*' means 'that'. (Appreciate the phonetic similarity). And '*tva*' means 'ness'. Hence, '*Tattva*' means 'thatness'. 'That' means 'the existence'. The existence of whatever 'is', is God. Being is God. It is this easy! It is such a fun!

Many difficult concepts started rapidly unfolding their meaning. Truth is everywhere, because whatever is, is Truth. These trees, this hill, this wind, these people, even this ant... all these are truth. "So all these are God?" And it flashed, "Yes, all these are God!" This is the meaning of the statements such as "God is everywhere" or in Sanskrit, *"Ishavasyam idam sarvam"* (the opening mantra of *Ishavasya Upanishad*, which means "Verily all this is God"). I had been reading this all along, I had been chanting this all along, and how is it that its simple meaning had never hit me directly?

A wonderful *haiku* in Japanese goes like this —

I said to a tree,
"Tell me about God!"
And the tree burst into a blossom.

The blossoming of the tree told what God is. The very 'is-ness' of that tree, the blossoming of that tree, is indeed God. All things in nature, day and night, are heralding by their very existence what God is. And that, God is!

And the meaning that I grasped while lying on the angioplasty table? After the big bang of creation, elementary particles were born out of that tremendous explosion of energy and they became the very substance of this universe. Everything in this universe is made up of the same electrons, protons and neutrons. So science does not doubt that one and the same truth permeates this Universe. In fact, to develop such an unified theory, 'General theory' which explains everything in the Universe is the ultimate goal of the modern physics. That theory would be a revelation of truth. Would it be the revelation of God?

Science and spirituality indeed go hand in hand!
I found one of Einstein's comments very captivating.

"A human being is part of a whole, called by us the 'Universe', a part limited in time and space. He experiences himself, his thoughts and feelings, as something separated from the rest -- a kind of an optical delusion of his consciousness. This delusion is a kind of prison for us, restricting us to our personal desires and to affection for a few persons nearest us. Our task must be to free ourselves from this prison by widening our circles of compassion to embrace all living creatures and the whole of nature in its beauty."

3.5

I continued reading books on spirituality. Completed reading the famous Patanjali's *Yog-sutras* along with the commentary on those *sutras*. I felt a strong urge to learn Sanskrit (however, I could never accomplish that). My main anchors were Vinoba's *Discourses on Bhagavad Gita* and his booklet *'Ishavasya vritti'.*

Ishavasya-vritti is worth its weight in gems and diamonds. *Ishavasya Upanishad,* the smallest (only 18 verses) of all Upanishads, propounds a philosophy that is very rich in content. Vinoba wrote a fitting commentary on it in the fewest possible words. And he did so on Gandhiji's request for personal use. The rich philosophy of *Ishavasya Upanishad,* an aspirant like *Gandhiji* and the preceptor like Vinoba, is a threefold confluence, whose sanctity is hard to match.

I recite *Ishavasya Upanishad* each morning. It is philosophically so rich that it moved Gandhiji to write, “If all books were to be destroyed and only one was to be saved, I will choose *Ishavasya Upanishad* for safekeeping.” When I recite in the morning, my mind feels clean and fresh like having taken a shower. The day feels like I were starting the life anew.

3.6

On getting the heart attack I had felt my life too short. It agonised and frightened me that my life might end soon. If and when death does approach me again, will I feel the same way? And why did I think that a life of 45 years up to that time was ‘short’? “The tragedy of life is not that it ends so soon, but that we wait so long to begin it.”

My act of living, I realised, consisted of a series of moments, but I had not lived a single moment fully. I began to notice that at any moment, while doing anything, I am thinking of something else. When I am in the shower, I am thinking of the speech I am going to give today, while eating a meal I am reading a newspaper, and while I am in the company of our family, I am thinking of rising prices. In fact, I do not live in that moment; I am engrossed in thoughts about some imaginary world. I have turned the physical act of living a given moment into a mental activity of thinking about that moment. Even when I am eating the most delicious chocolate I think, “How delicious! If only I could have more of this chocolate!” I actually live that thought about the chocolate; while the actual experience of the chocolate fades away in a background. Alienated from the experience of actually living any given moment, I complain that that there is no joy in life, or that life is too short. I began to understand my problem.

I wondered if I could master the art of living fully in that moment. I was a soul displaced from the moment, exiled from the moment of actual living. Suddenly a new word bloomed in my mind --

'kshana-stha!' -- anchored in the moment or living in the moment! (in Sanskrit, *'kshana'* means 'a moment'; the suffix *'stha'* connotes the 'location' -- so *'kshanastha'* means 'one who is located or anchored in a moment'). I need to be anchored in a given moment, we need to live that moment fully.

Every day I come out of the house early in the morning. I stand in the garden. A dim light begins to brighten up the horizon. Silhouettes of trees appear against the dim horizon. There is coolness in the air. A faint fragrance of flowers wafts along. I stand still taking all this in. I feel grateful. "I have received one more day, gift of grace this very moment. This is His piety and this is His gift. I had almost lost this life by my own deeds. And yet, I am alive *at* this moment. I am present *in* this moment. I am one with the nature surrounding me. I am a part of it. What lies without and what lies within are but one." A feeling of oneness with everything floods my mind. I am in complete unison.

Even one such moment is so rich and joyful that it suffuses the mind with the spiritual meaning of a line written by a Marathi poet: *"kshana eka pure premacha, varshava phado maranancha"* (A single moment of love is enough, then the deaths may rain.). But how often do we live a moment in this way? But was this moment a special moment? Or it was just like all other moments that make up my whole day. Only my heightened ability to fully experience a given moment enables me to live that moment much more, much deeper. Why can't this moment appear more often? Or it always does, but my eyes are waiting in anticipation of something else?

Is every moment so rich? So bursting with joy and romance? If it is, then it is pity that by not living it fully, I am simply wasting its enormous riches. I am the one who declines to receive the most joyful thing that each moment brings. And then I complain that life is short!

This moment is all that there is. We keep looking forward to something different, something 'out of this world', something absolutely thrilling and never taste the thrill of the present moment. I saw a very fitting cartoon. Two monks, one young and one old, are sitting side by side. The young monk is looking to a side, eagerly waiting for something extraordinary to happen, waiting for some divine revelation. The old monk says to him, "Nothing happens next. This is it!"

"Nothing happens next. This is it"
(Painter: Gahan Wilson. Publisher: *The New Yorker Magazine*, 1980)
(Figure 1)

A thought began to take shape in my mind -- if I master the art of fully experiencing and enjoying the given moment, it would be like a big bang of the moment. Like a nuclear explosion, a tremendous joy will be released from the explosion of every moment. But for that to happen, one must live with fully conscious awareness of the moment and not in the dreamland of thoughts. One would have to become *'kshanastha'*, i.e. anchored in a moment. Could I do it? All the techniques of *dhyana* essentially teach one to be sensitive to the experience of that moment, they teach one to become *'kshanastha'*. That is the goal of *dhyana*. If God is ever revealed in *dhyana*, that revelation must be in the form of the experience of truth due to one's heightened awareness of the truth residing in that moment.

However, all this is still on the intellectual level. I am not at the level of living fully in a moment. I have only seen a few glimpses of what it could be.

3.7

Today, I was getting ready to sit down for *dhyana*. I often use a flower as an object on which to focus the mind -- the so-called '*dharana*' in the yogic parlance. I picked a *champak* flower from the tree. Just one flower is enough for my practice. The *champak* flower! Its white beauty, the golden yellow hue at its centre and its unique fragrance suddenly transported me to my childhood forty years ago, weaving around me the memories of the very joyful and safe period in life. Holding a *champak* flower in hand is like sitting in a time machine! It transports me back to my childhood. A *champak* flower gives me two-fold joy.

Suddenly a thought popped up -- "What happened to my 'anchored-in-the-moment' state? Instead of experiencing the *champak* flower the way it is at this very moment, I am using it as a vehicle for re-experiencing my childhood!" The fragrance of the flower was a far more powerful medium than mere words; the sense of smell is far more primordial. Obviously, the sweet security of childhood was dearer to my mind, I loved the memories of my childhood more than the *champak* flower. But then, what of this flower I was holding? What of this moment? That moment was fleeting away. Wasted, lost!

I recovered; regained my lost balance. I did not want the *champak* flower to become a means of hiding myself in childhood. That flower is first and foremost a flower. It exists in this moment as a flower. The flower-ness of that flower is as much a truth as the truth of this universe. So that flower is truth, just as God is truth. The flower = truth = God! I must learn to live in the truth of this moment.

It began to dawn on me that *dharana,* the endeavour of looking at the flower with my entire attention focussed on it, is really a practice of experiencing the Truth of this moment or of living in this moment. *Dharana* is the study of the art and science of becoming anchored in this moment. Becoming anchored in the moment, becoming '*kshanastha*', is *dhyana.*

The *champak* flower became a vehicle of my spiritual journey!

A question arose in my mind today -- To be natural, to be non-artificial is like becoming what? Animals and plants are driven by natural instincts. Is becoming natural the same as becoming and behaving like animals?

In one of his poems, Nobel Laureate poet Octovia Paz says —

... But the butterfly
did not know it was a butterfly.
There was no thought in the mind of the butterfly.
It just flew.

Animals and plants lack awareness. Their behaviour is entirely natural, because the concept that they could behave in any other manner does not occur to them. Even though they live a natural life, they themselves have no awareness that they are living so. Living naturally without being aware of it cannot be a goal of human life. If that were to be the goal, then one could argue that becoming a lifeless rock and simply lying down motionless would be an even higher goal!

Man is propelled by natural drives just as the plants and the animals are; but apart from that, his imagination and his intellect suggest him something in addition. Man is a part of whatever is happening inside and outside him; and in addition, he is conscious of it. That is the greatest distinguishing feature of man. He is aware of the self. So man is Truth like a plant or a rock, but, besides that, he is a wakeful and self-conscious truth. Truth that is aware of itself is man!

Is this 'self-aware truth' the soul? Does *dhyana* awaken this self-awareness? Does this universe possess similar self-awareness? And if so, is cosmic self-awareness God? Is enlightenment the same as experiencing the oneness of individual self-consciousness and the cosmic self-consciousness?

*****

4. Revelation

"Why does man look for God? Why does man, in every nation, in every state of society, want a perfect ideal somewhere, either in man, in God, or elsewhere? Because that idea is within you. It was your own heart beating and you did not know; you were mistaking it for something external. It is the God within your own self that is impelling you to seek Him, to realise Him. After long searches here and there, in temples and churches, on earth and in heaven, at last you come back to your own soul, completing the circle from where you started, and find that He whom you have been seeking all over the world, for whom you have been weeping and praying in churches and temples, on whom you were looking as the mystery of all mysteries, shrouded in the clouds, is the nearest of the near, is your own self, the reality of your life, body and soul... By means of spiritual disciplines the individual soul ultimately recognises its oneness with the Universal Soul."

— Jnana Yoga

4.1

I continue to read and I experiment on my own self. As if, I have become a laboratory! Many aspects are unfolding.

* * *

I had a new experience today. The science of yoga describes *kumbhaka*[15], the pause between inhalation (called *'puraka'*[16]) and exhalation (called *'rechaka'*[17]). Yoga talks about three kinds of *kumbhakas* -- *'antar-kumbhaka'* (the pause at the end of inhalation), *'bahya-kumbhaka'* (the pause at the end of exhalation) and *'kevala kumbhaka'* (the spontaneous holding of breath). One cannot force a *'kevala kumbhaka'* to occur. If it occurs at all, it does so by itself, not by deliberate effort. I am still not adept at *'bahya-kumbhaka'*. It makes me gasp for air. But I managed the *'antar-kumbhaka'*, (holding still after inhaling) reasonably well. I had been practising it for many days and slowly prolonging the duration of time for which I could hold the breath in. Today, after taking a deep breath, I suddenly felt a certain sensation of utter peace during the few moments of *'antar-kumbhaka'*. It was as if the mind, devoid of any thoughts, had turned into a cloudless sky. It was the simple awareness of my sheer existence floating in space like a bird cruising up high with its wings fully spread out. There was no flutter, no ripple, no rustle, no bustle;

---

15. *Kumbhaka -- Pronounced as koom-buh-k(uh).*

16. *Puraka -- Pronounced as poo-ruh-k(uh). Literally, one that fills (the lungs) in.*

17. *Rechaka -- Pronounced as ray-chuck. Literally, one that empties out (the lungs).*

just peace, serene, translucent and quiet. This experience, lasting for ten to twelve moments after each intake of breath, was totally new. I had just gained a glimpse of why *kumbhaka* was so important.

***

Kumbhaka permitted a fleeting experience of peacefulness, but it would not last through the entire cycle of inhalation and exhalation. Sudden flashes of thought would interrupt the silence. Sometimes a train of thought and sometimes only a flutter of words like the tiny pieces of shredded paper fluttering in a breeze. A persistent cacophony of words cluttered my mind. I realised that they would not let me enjoy a state of silence and peace.

Why do these thoughts and words arise? I could see that they came needlessly crashing in uninvited. As soon as the slightest interlude of quietness and peace befell, these thoughts would bubble up from the very bottom of the mind. Thoughts. Messy, irrelevant thoughts, without any purpose, quite meaningless. They fatigued me. They frustrated me. And many times two thoughts would shoot out simultaneously, like two bleating public loudspeakers making an infuriating noise. A perpetual flourmill grinds out the words. But that is what my mind has been doing for a long time. It is a habit that dies hard.

These thoughts not only broke my concentration, but also displaced my awareness of the moment. I yearned for the experience of truth, but instead, these thoughts littered my mind. These thoughts were not the truth; they were mere bubbles of word-symbols someone had fashioned for verbally expressing the experience of truth. They were mere substitutes for the truth. They were forgeries. And they had turned against me like a Frankenstein. They flooded my mind and robbed me of an experience of truth.

And why did my mind crave to verbalise the experience rather than remaining immersed in that experience? I remember reading a Hindi novel written by Rajendra Yadav. The character of a writer in this novel says, "The writer in me never leaves me alone. He sits astride my neck and constantly nags me. My every moment is filled with one thought – 'How am I going to put this experience into words?' When my only son died and his body was about to be cremated, my mind thought – how shall I write this experience of grief?"

I looked inside me. Leave aside the other instances, but even when I was close to death on the angioplasty table, I had coined the word '*anu-visarjana*' (dissolution of body into atoms) for death. The memory took me back to April 18, 1995 – the day of my heart attack. After my chest pain in the morning, I was studying my own ECG. While I worried about the possibility of a heart attack, I also thought, "How awful! I have to look at my own ECG! This is like that Russian surgeon!" (I had read long ago about a Russian surgeon, who had, while being alone in the camp near the North Pole, suffered an attack of appendicitis. In order to stay alive, he had to operate on his abdomen by watching in the mirror.) A sentence had suddenly sprung in my mind, "My situation is like that of the Russian surgeon!" Indeed, even in the shadow of death, the mind does not let go of this habit of articulating words and sentences. As soon as the mind registers an experience, words follow like bubbles rising up from the bottom of a body of water. I must have an obsession of organising every experience in a tidy package of words! The habit of thinking had turned into a cancer of the mind! It was a parasite that drained away the peace of mind and robbed me of any opportunity to fully experience the experience!

And then it occurred to me – there is no organ called 'mind', in my body. This constant chaos of thoughts is what we call 'mind'. These thoughts and the reactions that follow these thoughts, the continuous train of brain waves, the electrical impulses that jump across the neural synapses are collectively known as 'mind'. The mind keeps me ever occupied; it tortures me. It is the root cause of my unease, disharmony and pain. It gobbles up every moment of my life. That moment is truth, the experience of that moment is truth. But I am not living in that moment. I am living in the verbalised reactions to each moment. Living? In fact, wasting my life!

I began to see that there is no peace, no ease, no 'living', unless these constantly rattling trains of thought are stopped. Will *dhyana* make them stop? How?

4.2

In fact, *dhyana* is not a field of intellectual activity. But my intellect was unwilling to sit quietly. It was trying to understand *dhyana* in its own rational ways. Gradually, I began to see the connections between the science of yoga and modern psychology. I read about the '*Rational Emotive Therapy*' (RET) developed by Albert Ellis, a world-renowned psychologist. According to him, our thoughts fashion our emotions and our behaviours. A thought is simply what we say to ourselves – a kind of self-talk. If we pay attention to this self-talk and consciously modify it, our emotional responses change appropriately. This was a very interesting insight that we reinforce our emotions by repeating to ourselves our pet sentences (such as "I am truly hapless", "I just cannot manage anything", "I would not be able to do that"). Listen to your own self-talk and you will understand how a sentiment gets moulded. Rephrase your sentences and your emotions will change too.

As I proceeded with my practice of *dhyana,* I saw that there was a lot of truth in what Ellis says. I started to experience it in my personal life. I was able to observe the close relationship between my thoughts and emotions.

How does my mind work? The mind cannot be seen from outside, but the behaviour, the actions and the gestures can be seen. Usually, emotions are the underlying cause of the actions. I shout angrily. Before the angry shouts and gestures, the emotion of anger has already flooded the mind. This angry emotion, an emotional distortion, or as Patanjali calls it, the *chitta-vritti,* can be experienced as sensations on the body. The emotion of anger can be experienced as a sensation of warmth felt in the ears, rapid breathing, a rustling sensation all over the body and a pounding in the head.

But how does anger arise in the mind? As we retrace the progress of our anger, moment by moment, we realise that something sparked off the explosion of anger. That spark could be a thought that had flashed in the mind, our own self-talk. Someone behaves in a manner that I disapprove. That usually does not directly arouse the feeling of anger. But it evokes a sentence or half a sentence in my mind like an actor speaking to himself on the stage, (an 'aside'). "This person has a low opinion about me!" That sentence works like a spark. The mind is already laden with the gunpowder; a sentence like this or some memory or some visual image from the past ignites the fuse, and people see my anger in terms of shouting. But, before that explosion occurs, a whole chain of events has already taken place in my mind in a fraction of a second.

External event → a thought in the mind/visual image → emotion → external action

The science of yoga assigns a high level of importance to the middle two links in this chain -- thoughts and emotions in the mind. Both yoga and psychology emphasize a control over these two links in our reactions to external stimuli. I began to understand how such a control or regulation might be achieved.

Patanjali said, "Yoga is *nirodha* (restraint, control) of *chitta-vritti*s, the movements, fluctuations of the mind." Freedom from the emotional responses arising in the mind is verily the yoga. But how does one become 'free' of these emotional responses? It does not happen by suppressing them. A suppression creates an internal stress, an internal pressure, which invariably explodes sooner or later. So how can *dhyana* help in this freeing?

A sudden spurt of emotion is often accompanied by physical sensations. Reactions of our body are always in sync with the prevailing emotion; be it anger, fear or a sexual desire. Reactions of our body are faithful and loyal reflections of emotions, hence Eckhart Tolle has described emotions as the reflection of mind in the body. Sometimes we suppress or deny the true nature of our feelings. Anger is generally regarded as undesirable, so I tend not to accept that I was angry. We can cheat our mind. But the responses of our body promptly betray what is really going on in the mind.

A method known as 'sensitivity training', developed at the National Training Laboratory, in the USA teaches how to recognise our true feelings. Some years ago I had received 'sensitivity training' in a training laboratory in India. If we pay very close attention to the thoughts arising in the mind and the accompanying physical manifestations, we can understand what is really going on in the mind. Suppose some event filled me with fear. Since I know that fear is a sign of weakness, I do not wish to accept that I am afraid. But a pit in the stomach and the sudden perspiration tell me the undeniable truth about the state of my mind.

This much I understood. But how to get freedom from an emotional storm or a harmful action resulting from it?

***

I attended the *vipashyana* retreat second time. This time it was more helpful than my first attendance. Some new nuances came to my attention.

Mind = (thoughts) + (reactions)
= (words, sentences, visual image) +
(breathing, sensation of chill, palpitations, etc.)

Analysing and then experiencing this division of 'mind' into two components helps us understand our mind.

In *vipashyana,* you learn to observe and experience the physical sensations that arise in your body. So, it is similar to the 'sensitivity training'. We experience our emotions or passions of our mind through the physical manifestations such as the rising up of hair, tremor, sensation of chill, a glow of warmth, sweat and changes in the breathing rate. We need to learn to quickly recognise them. But, simply observe them, not becoming involved with them. Do not let them snowball. We need to learn to detach from our mind and become an uninvolved spectator, an impartial witness. That will stem the chain of events that leads to an emotional outburst and resultant actions.

The self-talk that precedes the rise of an emotion and the accompanying sensation is the root cause of these distortions of the mind. We are usually unaware of this self-talk. It occurs almost at the subconscious level. Therefore, we remain unaware of the fact that a specific self-talk or a visual imagery and the subsequent chain of events have begun in the mind. *Dhyana*, be it *'anapana dhyana'* in the Buddhist system of *vipashyana* or the *dhyana* of the Patanjali's system of yoga, (Goutam Buddha and Patanjali were almost contemporary, nearly two and half thousand years ago) is a practice of observing and recognising, becoming conscious of what is going on at the subconscious level. Practice of *dhyana* thus means becoming aware about the transactions that occur at the subconscious level while we are fully awake and conscious. Great!

If I do not try to suppress the self-talk, but witness it consciously in 'real time'; if I 'see' it and recognise it; then the entire chain reaction of consequences arising from that self-talk will be stemmed. That seed sentence will simply arise and disintegrate without sowing the seeds of further events; I will remain totally detached.

This was becoming very interesting. The self-talk and the feelings that the self-talk evokes are like tidal waves. If, instead of letting myself drown in these waves I simply observe them like a witness sitting on the bank of the river, I remain free and safe from their storm-like destructive power. The thoughts come and go ceaselessly. That does not stop, but they become ineffective. Was this what Patanjali meant when he said "Yoga is the prevention/cessation of the ripples in the mind"? *Bhagavad Gita* also talks about a person whose mind is still (*sthita – prajnya*). A notion began to take shape in my mind that *Bhagavad Gita* is also referring to the same process of disabling the power of our thoughts to sway our mind. I could now understand, how the practice of yoga can help me attain such a state of mind. And I could relate that to my own mental states.

I realised that the science of yoga and modern psychology are very similar. Who would you admire? The practitioners of yoga who lived thousands of years ago and discovered this truth and developed a whole science to attain that; or the modern psychologists who rediscovered the same truth and developed modern scientific methodology based on it? I consider myself fortunate that both the traditions were accessible to me. In India, the confluence of the two mighty rivers Ganga and Yamuna is considered a holy place. I felt as if I was bathing in a confluence of two sacred rivers. Neither of them was alien to me. The Ganges is mine and so is Yamuna!

4.3

I yearned to see the light. "What will enlighten me? Should I go to the Himalayas and practise *dhyana* over there?" I used to muse. Once I wrote about this to Vimalatai. She wrote back, "The bondage is of the mind." The implication was clear -- the bondage exists in mind, but I was imagining the liberation from bondage to take place in the Himalayas. It only served to give my mind one more excuse -- "I have not gone to the Himalayas, I am still wrapped up with the affairs of this world, and therefore I cannot be free". The thousand games that our mind plays!

I continued my effort to understand these games of the mind. What happens when I sit down to practise *dhyana?* After a brief period of peace, a thought sneaks in. Another one follows on its heels. In the beginning, I am aware that these are only thoughts. Like scenes from a movie, they appear on the screen of my mind and disappear. But soon this awareness vanishes and I start to think of these thoughts as the reality. I begin to get engrossed in them. In sync with the swings of thoughts, my mind begins to generate reactions such as worry, happiness, anger, and so forth. In fact, I live inside my own mind far more than I live in the external world. Once the detachment towards the mind is lost, these internal thoughts seem real to me and I get trapped in their web. I become like little children, playing a game of mock fight but getting so absorbed in it that they really begin to fight over the imaginary things. What Vimalatai said is true -- the bondage exists only in the mind. Nowhere else is the bondage a reality.

When an actor recites his dialogue on the stage, he normally does not lose the awareness that it is a dialogue of a character, not his own thoughts. A heartbreak in the play does not prompt the actor to commit suicide in real life. On the stage of real life, I am also acting out the role of 'I'. This character speaks many dialogues to itself. These dialogues are what we call thoughts. As Albert Ellis says these thoughts are merely the sentences one speaks to oneself. They have no real, independent existence. And yet, how quickly we confuse them for reality! And how much we react to them! How easily we get tangled in their web! How much pain we suffer and how much pain we cause!

Dhyana is an exercise of observing these dialogues of the mind with studied indifference. Thoughts emerge, act their role out on the stage of the mind and disappear behind the curtain. The important thing is not to believe that these are 'my' thoughts, 'my' emotions. Assuming the role of a detached witness should stem the tide of all reactions. Observe the mind as if one is watching a play -- watch with great alacrity, but with the aloofness. J. Krishnamurti calls this a 'Choice-less awareness'.

What is expected from this? I noticed that the practice of *dhyana* slowly cultivated a new habit of mind. This habit begins to permeate and stay on during other hours of the day, other activities of the day. Without any fanfare and without any conscious effort, *dhyana* begins to influence all other moments of life. The habit of detachment calms down the tendency to be swayed by the external events and internal thoughts and emotions.

Yogic practice for liberation and enlightenment is a very effective mental exercise, a training of the mind. What do I do when I lie down in the posture of *'shavasana'*? I relax my body and keep my mind alert but stress-free. A stress-free body, a stress-free mind. This habit grows on you and starts to exert its influence at those hours when you are not practising *shavasana* or yoga. It brings a fresh and stress-free wakefulness to life.

The science of yoga instructs the seeker to focus his/her attention on some real object, an idol, a sound or the breathing in order to focus and steady the mind in one place. This is all right because these things constitute the truth. Focus on truth. Fine. But the thoughts that arise in the mind distract the attention. Then why is a seeker told to observe these thoughts? One is seeking the truth. Are these thoughts then the Truth?

It came to me all of a sudden that a thought has two distinct components. Arising of thought in the mind is a real event -- as real as breathing, as real as the sound that is heard and then fades away. That is why observing thoughts is one more method of watching the truth.

Arising of thoughts in the mind is a real event. But are the contents of those thoughts also the truth? It occurred to me that the content of each thought is not necessarily the truth. It could be sheer imagination or a distortion of reality. I may fancy that I am standing at the top of the Mount Everest. That I thought of such a thing is a fact, but my standing on the top of the Mount Everest is not. It is just a flight of fancy. That is why I ought to observe the content of a thought like a detached observer. Therein lies the freedom of the mind.

4.4

As I understood all this, I thought I was soon going to reach the stage of spiritual liberation. But alas! Mind is very deceptive. I ought to share with you my experience of yet another cycle of illusion.

I was striving to attain that, during the practice of *dhyana,* my ego should be quiet, thoughts should subside and I should experience a blissful peace and solitude. Sometimes I felt that I had made distinct progress towards this goal and felt highly pleased. But only a few days later the old nemesis would return. My thoughts would not subside, no matter which technique of *dhyana* I followed. There was no escape from the thoughts. Slowly, a sense of despondency began to take hold. “Where is that state of *dhyana*? Where is enlightenment, liberation and peace?” The mind began to wail in despair. How could it then be peaceful?

I read a lot, I searched a lot and I asked a lot of people. They did their best to answer my questions. But I had not had my own ‘experience’. I had not found my answer. There was this unending conflict in my mind. A new race had started; a new search had begun. It lasted for a long time -- for nearly a year and a half. On many occasions I ended up frustrated. I began to think that, maybe, the path of *dhyana* is not what I had hoped it to be. Should I quit? And then, one day, as if the switch was turned on. “What am I running after? What new craving has my mind generated? Even if this craving is for spirituality, as long as it is a craving, will it not make my mind restless? And is this craving truly spiritual or is it a new desire of the mind, simply a new illusion?

I could not empty my mind of all thoughts, because that is unnatural. Thoughts are the food of the mind. Thoughts are the sustenance of the mind. Mind is nothing but a ceaseless flow of related - unrelated thoughts. How could then mind be free of thoughts?

Words and sentences that well up in the mind are what we call thoughts. But they don’t arise alone. Feelings accompany these words and sentences. Reactions rooted in the memories of old experiences are the feelings. Pleasant with some sentences and unpleasant with others. That we desire some things and that we do not desire other things is the complex of love-hate relationship. Thoughts are not the impediment to spirituality. The real impediment is the love-hate reactions that accompany these thoughts. Our reactions are the impediment. We need liberation, not from thoughts, but from our reactions of like, dislike and yearning that follow these thoughts. Sage Patanjali said, "Yoga is the prevention of our reactions, passions." He did not say "Prevent your thoughts!" The teaching of *anapana* meditation in *'vipashyana'* is also the same -- "do not get involved in the thoughts that arise in the mind, simply observe them, be totally neutral towards them." This is like sitting on the bank of a river and simply watching it flow by, not jumping into it, not getting caught up in the current, not getting sucked into the whirlpool. Do not try to stop the flow of the river of thoughts. If you try, you will be acting against the very nature of things. It will create more turbulence, build up pressure against the wall you put up and will finally break that wall down. It is far better to learn the art of pulling yourself out of the thought-river, and sit on the bank to simply observe the flow.

It is impossible to stop thoughts and sensations or to prevent their emergence; it is a futile effort. If one engages in that, that effort itself becomes a new craving and defeats the very purpose of the efforts – liberation from all cravings! To witness your thoughts without getting sucked in their whirlpool is *vipashyana*. And *dhyana* is in essence the practice of witnessing your thoughts without getting involved in them. *Dhyana* is essentially not a practice of concentrating your total attention on a single thing, (that is called '*dharana*') nor is it a devoted effort to reach a thoughtless state of mind. And it certainly is not a project for attaining revelation. It is simply practising the art of detached watching.

The puzzle was thus solved one day and I realised that I had been chasing a mirage. That was the source of my new dissatisfaction. I had been battling against an illusion, shadow-boxing against something which did not exist and therefore there was no hope of winning! The solution was to quit fighting and to understand that one had been fighting an illusion. The illusion vanishes, the battle is over!

Vimalatai Thakar, Vinoba Bhave, J. Krishnamurti and Mr. S. N. Goenka (the modern day teacher of *vipashyana*) had all said the same thing. They had indeed provided the answers and I had read them. However, my mind was not ready to receive their answers. To continue the effort without losing hope is *sadhana*. It would be a gross error to say that I realised this answer through my efforts. When one strives ceaselessly, it brings on fatigue, it opens one's eyes, it makes one humble and surrender. The answer silently blooms in one's mind when the mind is filled with the attitude of humility.

I sensed a certain growth in my clarity. The unrealistic expectations about liberation and revelation began to ebb away and the hankering of my mind began to abate. Now there was less confusion, less doubt. I was able to see the path more clearly. I knew the where and how of my journey. All that was needed now was to follow that path with unwavering practice. The *sadhana*.

4.5

I must tell what happened and what did not happen as a result of my practising yoga.

I do not know whether the practice of yoga leads to the vision of the Divine as imagined based on what one reads in scriptures and other writings. But it certainly benefits the practitioner on the physical and psychological levels. I can say from my own experience that it makes the body healthy, it makes the mind joyful and it makes life abloom with a distinct freshness. Now why should the practice of yoga deliver such valuable gifts?

Remember that blissful innocence of childhood, the passion of adolescence and the vigour and optimism of youth? These that made life bristle with newness and freshness. How easy it was to feel a sense of closeness with a rabbit, a parrot or a dog when we were children! It was easy to feel one with them when we were not constantly engaged in nursing our ego. The intense sensitivity of youth gave us special powers. I remember, one day I was cycling to the college and I suddenly heard the voice of Lata[18] -- a song was playing on a radio set in one roadside shop. I felt as if I was touched by something divine. That divine sensation entered through my ears and made every chord in my body vibrate like the strings of a *tanpura*[19]. The whole world was bathed in a glimmer of light. I stopped, got off my bicycle and just stood still, my mind floating on the notes of Lata's song, my mind awash in the lightened up world around me. So acute was my capacity to be touched by a single note of a song when I was young! That was when I was highly optimistic about bringing justice and happiness to the entire world. I was ready to throw my life for the worthy causes. This intense sensitivity, this ability to resonate nourished and enriched my life as a young man.

As life proceeded, my ego began to get more pronounced. Gradually and unknowingly, a division of my world occurred into 'I' and 'mine' on one side and 'everything else' on the other side. The sensitivity towards life became dim. I accepted it as 'maturity', 'wisdom of age' and 'practical mindedness'; but the juices were drying up.

Practice of yoga made those juices of life flow again! It refreshed everything. I am inclined to believe that the practice of yoga and *pranayama* brings on such a transformation because they enable you to stay awake and be sensitive, to the very essence, the 'is-ness' of every moment. The statement, "This is it, nothing happens next!" is

---

18. *Lata -- Lata Mangeshkar, the most celebrated female singer of India.*

19. *Tanpura -- A string instrument, used as an accompaniment in Hindustani classical music.*

the essence of the teaching of yoga. The awareness of this moment, this breath, this sensation, is the ultimate truth of this moment. Yoga makes the mind aware so that it can fully receive the truth of the moment. Practice of yoga is learning to sense the subtlest experience of every moment, a sensitivity training. It enables the practitioner to see Truth, with this body and with these eyes, in this moment and in every moment. (Is this is what they refer to as 'revelation' and 'vision'?) One begins to find happiness in reality, in the things and events just as they are; one is rejuvenated. Even if you keep aside the claim that yoga is a path to the spiritual, 'other-worldly' experience, the fact remains that yoga does bring joy and elevation of spirit on the psychological and physical levels in this world. And how does a joyful mind help? Vinoba once made a beautiful statement -- "That the mind will become joyous when all suffering has ceased is an illusion. When the mind will become joyous all suffering will cease!"

As the person becomes integrated, so does his world. As he feels good, so does the world look good — Abraham Maslow.

* * *

Different techniques of *dhyana* increase the sensitivity of different sensory organs. Some techniques focus on increasing the sensitivity of sight *(trataka)*, some focus on sound i.e. the sensitivity of hearing (*shravana)*, some focus on the experience of touch *(vipashyana)* and some others focus on transactions of the mind. It is my personal experience that *dhyana* increases the sensitivity of all the sensory organs and also enhances the intensity of sensory perceptions. Colours of the very same flower appear more vivid and hold the attention more firmly. The same note or sound touches a deeper chord.

But this is merely an enhancement of the sensory experiences. (And in the West, the instructors of 'sensuality' training have indeed been using such techniques as a means of enhancing the bodily pleasures). Vimalatai has often cautioned that what is usually taught as *'dhyana sadhana'* is an exercise of concentration. It is useful, but that itself is not *dhyana*. Vinoba has gone further, and said, "I do not support the claim that the process or practice of *dhyana* in itself is spiritual, because it can also be used for obtaining the pleasures and powers in this material world as well. Therefore, unless it is yoked to the devotion of Divine, *dhyana* does not become spiritual."

* * *

It is somewhat embarrassing to share in great a detail about one more of my experiences during this period. However, as the eminent psychologist Carl Rogers says, "Things we consider most personal, are the most general!" Nothing is private, unique; most experiences of a human being are universal, to most human beings. Since sexuality belongs to this category, I assume that what I have to tell is pertinent to all.

I am a man. Therefore, apart from all the social influences to which I have been exposed since birth, I am a male on the purely biological level. In childhood, in adolescence and in youth, that biological male identity was always alive and kicking inside me. I am also a married man and I have experienced all the joys and frustrations of a married man. I have experienced the intensity of sex drive and desires. Even though I grew up in the ashrams of Gandhiji and Vinoba, I never regarded *brahmacharya*[20] as my goal. Due to my education in medicine in India and abroad and the influence of Western thought on my psyche, I have always regarded sex as a necessary life force, an important factor in human life. So I willingly accepted the swings of my sexual desires and the accompanied joys and sorrows.

As I embarked upon the practice of *dhyana, pranayama* after

---

20. *Brahmacharya -- The conventional meaning of brahmacharya is abstinence from sex. I, as a translator of this book chose to use the original Sanskrit word here for reasons that will become apparent by the end of this section.*

my bout with the heart ailment, my sex drive began to ebb away, unbeknownst to me, without any conscious efforts to drive it away. The intensity of sexual desire or passion diminished. The frequency diminished. Slowly my biological identity as a male calmed down a little. Earlier, there used to be a 'charge' of sexuality around all the events and experiences in my life. Not that I did not want that aura of sensuality. But if it gradually began to grow dim, I do not know whether this was good or bad; nor did it depend upon what I willed or wanted. But one thing it did for me was that I began to see the world around me more objectively without the ever-present tint of sexuality. The passions and fluctuations in relationships grew weaker.

Just as I do not know whether this was good or bad, I do not know for sure why it happened at all. Was it the result of my middle age? Was it because of my diabetes? Was it a side effect of the beta-blocker medicines I was consuming? Or was it the effect of changes in my diet? Could it have been brought upon by the practice of yoga and *dhyana*? Usually, the regimens such as changes in diet, exercise, *dhyana* and reading of scriptural texts are prescribed for the unerring observance of *brahmacharya*. I was following those regimens as a means of protecting myself from heart disease. However, I noted that these regimens had affected my sex drive. Surely there must be a connection between the two. I felt the need to read and to understand what Gandhiji has written on this topic in his booklet *'Mangal Prabhat'* -- "Every one ought to remember what *brahmacharya* really means. It means to practise a behaviour consonant with the quest for *brahman*, or the ultimate Truth. Mastery of all senses is a special meaning that is derived from the original meaning of *brahmacharya*. It would behove everyone to forget the grossly incomplete and insufficient notion that *brahmacharya* is nothing more than the abstinence from sex."

4.6

I ought to also tell what *dhyana* did not do for me. I have not been able to completely empty my mind, nor have I been able to make my mind absolutely still. And I have not experienced what is termed as a *samadhi*.

Though I received a healthy and a joyful state of body and mind through the practice of *yoga* and *dhyana*, I still find that the aberrant straying of my mind continues. I understood at the intellectual level what the ancient sages of India meant by *'soham'* (identification of oneself with the cosmic principle, so that one is truly one with everything else in the universe). However, that intellectual understanding has not reached the emotional level, my attitude towards everything around me, or my behaviour. The closer I look at this cage of my ego, the stronger it appears to break. Though I know that the separation of 'I' from everything else in the universe is a mere illusion, that knowledge alone is not sufficient to break down the cage of 'I' and 'mine'.

And how strong is this cage! How irrevocably it separates me from the rest! When I was named 'Abhay' in my childhood, each time I heard that name being pronounced, each time people around me described this 'Abhay' and each time people passed judgements on this 'Abhay', a bar of this cage was firmly put in place. Each bar around me increased my separation from others and from the rest of the universe. And this cage, built around me without my awareness, without my willing or consent, had now become unbreakable. It has become a reference standard against which I now evaluate every event, every person. And this happens long before I know it. It has become a 'reflex action'. My intellect may repent afterwards, but my reflexes defer to 'I' and 'mine'. I can see the bird of my mind fluttering inside this cage, I can see it repeatedly bumping against its walls and falling down. I can see this all. And yet the ego stands undiminished. *Dhyana* has not liberated me from my ego. Elimination of ego and the attachment to 'mine', and the realisation of oneness with the universe is my liberation. How will that state be attained? When?

Ishavasya Upanishad says, "There is no illusion and no grief for that knower whose soul *(atman)* is one with all the elements of this universe, who sees and experiences only the eternal oneness." But the mind does not settle in such awareness of universal oneness and liberation. Intellectually, I know what this universal oneness is, but how will it become one's permanent state of mind?

Is it due to my personal inadequacy? I hesitate to say; perhaps those who claim to be or are touted as being the 'accomplished ones' in this field will be hurt. But I have observed that many who practise yoga, are also possessed by their own likes and dislikes, jealousies, affections and hatreds, egos and anger. One could, of course, argue that these people have not reached the high level of perfection, and therefore, evidence of such people cannot be used to infer that this is a limitation of yoga per se. Hence, I will not generalise. I am not interested in judging others. I wanted to clean my own pot; it was not getting any cleaner. I was rubbing it harder and harder, but the stains would not come off. My mind did not get cleansed.

I began to think that though the knowledge and practice of *dhyana* are useful and important, love and devotion are vital for cleansing the mind, for cultivating an attitude of purity, humility and generosity. Love liberates man from the bondage of selfish interests and unites him with others; and devotion (*Bhakti*) bonds him to God and to the whole universe. So it is important to transform the intellectual understanding and *dhyana* into devotion to God. Only then will one attain a state described by Saint Tukaram -- I have become as tiny as a molecule and as enormous as the sky!

4.7

Though now my intellect knew the answer, my heart remained unsatisfied. Why and where does this hankering arise? What is lacking? My soul was still searching.

Two books written by one of the greatest psychologist Eric Fromm, *'Man for Himself'* and *'Art of Loving'*, are almost advocates of spirituality. Fromm says that as long as man was as ignorant as the flora and fauna of the earth, he had no problems. But when, during the course of evolution, he realised that he was in some ways different from nature, his status became greatly elevated. And at that very moment he became separated from the rest of the natural world at the level of awareness. Having thus left the womb of creation, he suffers the pain of loneliness, separateness and alienation. But he cannot return to the mother's womb and once again attain the state of not-knowing. He has no pathway to return there. He can only go forward. The greatest spiritual challenge for man is to find a cure for this separation and alienation.

Fromm suggests that love is the cure. Love joins the alienated, lonely human to other humans and solves the original problem. That is why love is man's primary need, man's basic hunger. Love between human beings, love between humans and animals, love between humans and the environment is the cure for alienation.

The Greek mythology tells the story of King Midas. King Midas wanted to be very rich. He asked God for a boon -- anything I touch should turn to gold! God told him not to ask for such a boon, but Midas was insistent. "So be it!", said God. Midas was very pleased. He came into the palace. He touched a bowl of copper and it turned to gold. He touched a chair and it turned to gold. He touched the bed and it turned to gold. Soon there was a huge pile of gold. Midas's joy knew no bounds.

Midas was hungry. An attendant brought him a plate with delicious food piled on it. As soon as Midas touched the food, it turned to gold. He touched a glass of water and it too turned to gold. Midas sat in front of a pile of gold, hungry and thirsty.

Modern man is like King Midas. Since he has found the golden touch of science and technology, he can create wealth wherever he goes. But there are hardly any relationships. So he remains emotionally hungry and thirsty. Success, progress, wealth -- they are but a mirage and no matter how long he chases this mirage, he can never satisfy his thirst, because the thirst is for love, for relationship.

Just as the North Pole of a magnet seeks out the South Pole, man seeks for a mate at various levels. The void in the heart is filled by the relationship of love between man and woman, and by friendships. From this point of view, all spiritual practices are also a search for a mate. Human soul seeks out the cosmic soul. A devotee yearns to be one with God. The word 'yoga' is derived from the Sanskrit verb *'yuj'*. *'Yuj'* means to join. Yoga and *dhyana* bestow upon the practitioner an experience of oneness and free him from the tyranny of separation.

Why does one experience peace and joy while practising *dhyana*? In a state free of stress and strain, the disturbances caused by one's desires and wants are absent. There is nothing to be done during that sitting. Then one is aware only of the existence of one's own self and that of the universe. In this state, the individual ego is in embrace with the cosmic soul. It is an embrace without any ripples of passion or desire. The ties that cause stress are undone, loneliness is over and what remains is only the experience of being one with the universe. That is what bestows the blessing of peace and joy.

* * *

What exactly are the fear of death and desire to be alive? Today I started thinking. What are we afraid of losing at the time of death? This body? The limbs and organs of this body? I stared at them. Is this hand me? What if the hand were to burn away without a trace of pain? In my mind, I chopped my limbs one by one and burned them away. To my surprise, I could not imagine any pain, grief or sadness. My hand was on fire and I watched it burn like a log of wood! I felt certain that love of life could not be same as love for my limbs or the collection of limbs and organs that we call 'body'. Surely I need this body to live, it is useful to me for living, but this body is not life!

Is love of what I own the same as love of life? I did not own those things in the past and even then I desired for life. And I will want to live tomorrow even if these things are gone. So what exactly is life that I lust for?

And then it came to me -- it is the experience of living that I lust for. A cassette of music in itself is not a thing of joy. It is the experience of listening to music that is joyful. Owning this cassette is only an assurance that I will be able to listen to music at will. But I often forget that and get very attached to this cassette, to things and to this body. The body and the material things are surrogates, mistaken for the real living. A little reasoning dispels the illusion. *One loves not the instrument of living, but the act of living, the experience of living*.

But what is 'an experience of living'? At the moment of that experience, what exactly happens that I long for it again and again? Sensory organs such as eyes and ears experience pleasant sensations of sight and sound, but what makes those sensations pleasant? We meet people that we like and the moments of their company are very desirable to us. Why?

Aha! *Life is a continuous series of experienced relationships.* These are my relationships with people, things, sounds, memories and ideas. The experience of these relationships is what I desire. Life is an experience of these relationships. So what is desirable is not this body, not these things, but the experience of relationships obtained by means of the body and the things.

That started clarifying some things. This relationship or love is what frees one from the cage of loneliness, even if for a few moments. And that is why it is desirable, nay, essential. When there is no relationship, no connection, no love, man's life becomes lifeless garbage and it kills him. The power of love is a blessing. Whether someone will love us or not is not within our power, but it is certainly within our power to love someone. So the key to living is in our own hands!

Some individuals possess this power, this ability to love. They can easily connect with others emotionally. Their problem is solved immediately. But most people lose this ability. While chanting the mantra of 'I', 'mine' and 'to me', the 'I' becomes separated from everyone else. How can there be a salvation for those who cannot forget or transcend the 'I', those who are incapable of connecting and becoming one with others?

This was not just a philosophical question for me. It was my problem! My personal as well as existential problem. I was haunted for years by a nagging awareness of this problem but today I had put my finger on it. I wondered whither lay my salvation.

Those ancient Indian sages who developed a pathway to spirituality must have been as accursed as I was. Out of this necessity they must have discovered a pathway to becoming one with the universe. There are two ways to free oneself from the cage of one's own ego -- spiritual awakening and love. Spiritual awakening can occur on various levels by various pathways -- on the intellectual level by way of reason and reflection, on the level of awareness by means of *dhyana* and on emotional level through the path of devotion. An aspirant can liberate himself/herself from the loneliness in the cage of the 'I' by following any of these three pathways depending upon his/her attitude and ability.

4.8

I cannot sustain the state of spiritual awareness for long and soon I return to the world of my ego, my ambition, my dissatisfaction, pain and suffering. I feel like the spider in the children's tale that keeps trying to scale a wall and keeps falling down. How can I sustain the spiritual awareness at all times? I am not one of those 'liberated souls' to whom God revealed himself. Must I forever keep climbing up and falling down?

This question often bothered me. Hope could be one answer -- a hope that one day I will reach my destination. I discovered as alternative -- there is no 'place to be reached', no destination to arrive at. This journey, this climbing up and falling down, is in itself the destination of each moment. *Nothing else happens, nothing else will ever happen. Whatever 'happens' within me and around me is itself the revelation! To realise this truth is the enlightenment.*

There is one more path for attaining a permanent state of oneness with the universe -- devotion to the Divine Principle. The lasting awareness of one-ness attained by those who follow the path of *jnyana* (reason and contemplation) and the path of *dhyana* can also be attained by the path of devotion, (*bhakti*). By 'devotion to the Divine Principle', I do not imply a naiveté or blind faith or an observance of rituals and rites. What I am referring to is the ability to perceive the presence of God everywhere at all the times and to bring one's behaviour in concordance with that perception. I fail to achieve that feat. The intellect and ego are the two major impediments. What is needed is a total surrender of my ego, a sacrifice of my ego. But I do not have what it takes to surrender or sacrifice the ego. When I read the devotional poetry of Saint Tukaram, I realised how tall and intense his devotion to God was and that brought tears to my eyes. The majestic sight of the Himalayas makes one acutely aware of one's own smallness and it makes one feel humble. That is exactly how I feel whenever I read Saint Tukaram's devotional songs.

So after all, I do have one last resort. If the paths of *dhyana* and *jnyana* do not liberate me, the path of devotion is the final resort. What the reason and effort cannot achieve, devotion and surrender will. But to attain that attitude, the ego will have to be washed away. As Saint Kabir has said,

With soap and water the body can be cleaned

But how clean can it be if the stains within remain?

* * *

Today I read a *bhajan* (hymn) composed by Saint Kabir. It totally overwhelmed me. "This indeed is the answer to my ever torturing problem!" I thought –

O Seeker! Simple is the path of spirituality
Do not close your eyes nor plug the ears
You need not give your body the slightest torture

With open eyes recognise and behold with smile
His beautiful face all around.

Wherever you go, let it be a walk around Him
Whatever you do, let it be service to Him.

Lying down to sleep is prostration humble
Offer no other worship, It is just that simple.

Whatever you utter, His chant; whatever you hear, His name
What you eat and what you drink – an offering to his fame

One and same are the home and wilderness
See no difference, no separateness.

Engrossed in Eternal Word, merciful'n kind
Shed all evil desires away, far and far behind.

In waking or in sleep, ceaselessly I experience
Most joyous note, an unbroken trance.

— *Kabir*

How can every moment of life become an offering to God and one never needs to sit down to practice *dhyana* with eyes and ears shut? How can the Divine Principle be seen all around one? *Kena Upanishad* says, "Through every sensory experience and through every intellectual transaction the Almighty must be known, realised and experienced." To be meaningful, God could be realised here and now, in this body and with these eyes.

I am still searching. Sometimes the yearning is strong. I feel that the whole day is gone, but I have not experienced that state. Sometimes I feel peaceful. Sometimes I feel His presence, even if only for a few moments. This is an assurance. As Saint Tukaram says, "He who stands for a moment at God's doorstep attains liberation."

4.9

Today I got tired of calming down the constant unruly behaviour of my mind while I was trying to see Him by way of *dhyana*. I thought, "This is not for me! Yoga and *dhyana* help maintain the physical health and a joyful, pleasant, relaxed attitude. That the practice of yoga and *dhyana* restores beauty to life and lifts the burden off one's mind is a great benefit, but it does not lead to a vision of God. At least it does not work for me in that manner. I should leave this path and follow a different path. Perhaps the path of devotion will help me."

I was obsessed with this thought for a couple of weeks, but continued with the practice of *dhyana*. One day a new significance of *dhyana* dawned on me. Various techniques of *dhyana* render various sensory organs more sensitive and those sensations become increasingly clarified and attain a high level of purity. The practice of 'sight-*dhyana*' cleanses the faculty of seeing. The practice of focussing attention on the sense of touch (*vipashyana*) makes the sense of touch keener and cleaner. It is easy to understand that the sense of touch gets keener. But how does it become 'cleaner'? After all, we comprehend what the skin senses only with the help of our mind. If the mind is turbulent, the high level of noise garbles the signal coming from a sensory organ. Mind's own noise adds confusion to the signal. *Dhyana* helps the mind become neutral and objective. That eliminates, or at least lessens any distortion in the perception.

The world around me is the Truth. The means that I have for understanding and comprehending it are my sensory organs and my mind. Therefore Vinoba calls these, the doors of the body that let the light in. To make these instruments sensitive and clean is to develop the faculty of perceiving Truth as is. *Dhyana* and yoga help us perceive the Truth more clearly. As I have narrated earlier, I had already accepted that Truth is God. And a high fidelity perception of the universe = vision of Truth = the vision of God!

Once again I had gone the whole circle of clarification and purification of my faculty of 'seeing' and I was able to see clearly. I understood how *dhyana* takes one closer to God. *There is no God external to this universe. Dhyana enables the practitioner to 'see' God in whatever exists and happens all around at that very moment. That is the vision of God! That is revelation!*

There is no separate God outside this universe. The universe is brimming with God. God does not have to come from somewhere outside so that I can see him. When my 'vision' is clean, clear and keen, He will become visible to me where He is and as He is. God will have to become installed in my vision and my vision will have to be instilled with God. This is yoga; this is devotion.

"Let the Divine accompany wherever the mind wanders!", says one saint.

* * *

My day begins with singing of *Ishavasya Upanishad* in early morning. It says, *Poornamidah* (That, Divine Principle, is infinite and complete), *Poornamidam* (This manifest universe is also infinite and complete).

This morning as I recited this mantra, it occurred to me that I am able to accept that the attribute-less, un-manifested Divinity is complete in itself. But, it is not easy for me to accept that the manifest universe that surrounds me is also complete in itself and just as divine. I have a hard time experiencing Divinity in this world. This fully morphed, attribute-rich universe elicits a love-hate and a like-dislike reaction from me. The notion of God as a formless, attribute-less abstract principle appeals to me; it suits my temperament. Since that entity has no form and no attributes it elicits no reaction from me, I can accept it. But the manifest and fully formed world does generate a like-dislike reaction in my mind.

And here is a real conflict. Those who follow the path of devotion to a manifest deity say that worshipping an abstraction is hard, so a manifest form is essential for realising, worshipping God. But my experience is exactly the opposite. When will I be able to see Divinity that exists in the concrete, manifest forms? When will I experience what *Ishavasya Upanishad* says -- *'Ishavasyam idam sarvam'* (All this manifested is permeated by Divinity)? When will that become my lasting experience?

This yearning, this unrelenting quest as to when I realise the Divine is a constant agony in my path to spirituality. In reality, that vision of Divine is all around me at this very instant! Only I cannot see it, I cannot feel it. When shall I receive the gift of that vision? When will this curtain between the Truth and I be lifted?

* * *

Idol worship was simply appalling to me. I had almost never engaged in idol worship. Rani loves to worship an idol. Though I never opposed her, I used to make fun of her from time to time. I hated the rituals and rites that accompany idol worship. To me, the notion of an invisible Divinity that permeates the entire universe was far more satisfying than imagining that God is residing in one little idol. So my worship, if you call it worship, was a worship of the formless, nameless, attribute-less abstract Divinity.

This was also a part of my psyche. I could relate less with a person of flesh and blood than the person's biological, psychological or spiritual principle. The disease of the patient, rather than the patient himself or herself, held my interest. I found the concept of humanity more appealing than relating with a human being. Since I was conditioned far more by the rational thought than by emotions or sentiments, I was naturally drawn towards the notion of a formless, nameless, attribute-less God.

In the 10th, 11th and the 12th chapters of his commentaries titled *'Talks on Gita'*, Vinoba has discussed in detail the topics of idol worship, worship of a manifest God and the worship of an un-manifested God. When I read Vinoba's explanations of these ideas, my objections founded upon the so-called rational thought began to weaken. Vinoba's commentaries are so unparalleled that one ought to read them in their original form. According to him, the Divine Principle (Truth Principle) permeates an idol just as it permeates the entire universe, so the idol is a microcosm of the universe. Though diminutive, an idol is still a complete form, not a tiny incomplete fraction of God. It is a small print edition, not a piece. That explained the idea behind idol worship a little bit to me.

I found Saint Jnaneshvara even more fascinating. If an idol is a microcosm i.e., representative of the universe, Saint Jnaneshvara dignifies an even more easily accessible symbol, the word form -- God's name! *Jnaneshvara* tells how beneficent is God's name —

"Hold to the single principle of God's name with steadfast devotion, surely God will be merciful to you"

Or

"There is no other principle like the principle of God's name, following any other path is wasteful"

Or

"Remembering God's name bears the fruit; it turns everything around you into God's abode"

This philosophy was totally incomprehensible to me and yet it filled me with an acute sense of curiosity and wonder. Starting with the notion that 'this universe is not an illusion, the universe is the body of God', the sages had proceeded to envision the universal divinity in an idol and then to realise it in God's name. That such a feat is possible was appealing to my reason and emotion both, though I have not internalised it as my faith. And from where shall I acquire the attitude of faith that is needed for it?

* * *

My intellect has understood and I can see clearly. And yet that feeling does not last, my mind cannot stay anchored in that awakening. When I think of God, when I think of Truth, it is as if a current of energy flows through my body. I realise that the same Divine Principle – Truth – is everywhere. When I recite *Ishavasya Upanishad*, all the doubts vanish and the Truth comes into a sharp focus. But why does this state not last all day long? When I am engrossed in other thoughts and in my daily activities, my mind assumes an attitude pertinent to that situation and it no longer stays anchored in God-awareness. So, a mere intellectual understanding is not useful; that awakening must become a lasting state of mind. The mental attitude must change.

I have reached the very edge of the terrain of intellect. I can see the land that lies beyond, but my intellect cannot take me there. My confidence in my faculty of reasoning and my ego are getting weaker. I ask, "Why is it that my intellect, which is very useful in every other aspect of life, is too feeble to carry me beyond? What vehicle do I have that will take me across?" I want that God-awareness to become a permanent state of mind. I want that attitude, that awakening, that vision; not just an intellectual knowledge.

I am at the very doorstep of devotion. But I cannot bring myself to step into that suite. The mind is reluctant to let go of the reason. It fears and hesitates. My feet grow weak. I can see what lies beyond, but cannot force my feet to saunter across. How can there be a true God-awareness without the surrender of devotion?

4.10

I detested the rituals and rites that accompanied '*upasana*', the worship. In my eyes it was an irrational, blind faith. My highest ideal was rationality. I regarded anything that was not rational as a debasement. I hated the rituals and the offerings of leaves, flowers, grains of rice and lamps and all the hocus-pocus.

Of late, I began to question this position. Is this a blind faith or is this a symbolic worship? Did I believe that an expression of sentiments and thoughts in the form of symbols is a trashy notion? I had accepted so many symbols of modern times! In chemistry I had learned that the letter 'H' was the symbol of hydrogen. Though I knew that the letter 'H' was not in itself the hydrogen gas, I used it as a symbol of hydrogen. I understood all the chemical formulae and equations using such symbols and reached correct answers. And is not the entire arena of words and language a land of symbols? If I accepted a flag as a symbol of my nation, why was it illogical to me to accept an idol or a flower as a symbol? There could be no objection to accepting a symbol as long as one is mindful that a symbol itself is not the thing it represents. When that mindfulness is lost, blind idol worship begins. Events like feeding an idol of Lord Ganesha a glass of milk are celebrated; erecting statues or smashing them become major political issues. If one can harbour and nurse the sentiment that an idol represents the Divinity of the entire universe, an idol ought to be acceptable as a means. Representing Divinity through an idol seemed to me as a very intelligent instrument fashioned by the culture.

I also began to understand that in the market-oriented, pleasure-seeking modern-day culture, even relationships, emotions and commitments to values have been reduced to the level of commodities. Commodities can be bought and commodities can be thrown away. Everything is becoming a thing to be exploited. Nature, land, forest, air, sky, all are 'commodities'. Even God is a commodity! Use it when needed and throw it away as soon as the need is over! But making everything a commodity delivers neither the joy nor the satisfaction. No matter how many such new commodities are collected; their innate worth, their essence is getting lost and these commodities are turning into a lifeless trash.

Contrary to this, the older cultures followed a different path. They endowed the ' things' with 'sentiment'. They invested the idols with a divine meaning. They invested a thread around the wrist with the sentiment of a sister[21]. They made a leaf, a flower, a coconut and *kumkum* the instruments of worship.

In childhood, I had stayed at my aunt's place in a small village for a year. She was an old-fashioned lady. We were playing with the other children in her household and someone unknowingly knocked down a glass tumbler, shattering it. My aunt grieved over it. "I have had that glass tumbler for 18 years!", she lamented. A question such as "Is that cheap little glass tumbler, used for 18 years, still valuable to you?" would have been totally out of line. What it cost to buy was not the issue. It was no longer a 'thing' for her. It had become, in my aunt's way of thinking, an entity that had its own personality, its own right to exist. That glass tumbler deserved a 'human right' to exist. My aunt was upset with us because we had violated the rights of that glass tumbler to exist!

That glass tumbler meant something to her. She and the culture she had grew up in had attributed that significance to a mere glass tumbler. Oxen, cows, trees, leaves, rivers, all had a special meaning in that culture. And they all had an emotional and spiritual significance over and above their material worth.

Not only material objects, but also the actions have significance on a different level. Many years ago, I had visited the city of Kyoto

---

21. *There is an annual ceremony called 'rakhi-bandhana' (tying of a band of threads by a sister on the brother's wrist) which is performed in every Hindu household. It represents sister's love for her brother and serves to remind the brother that he has a duty towards her.*

in Japan. A housewife had performed the well-known Japanese 'tea ceremony' for us there. This is a very intricate form of hospitality. Every movement, every action of the hostess performing the tea ceremony, had a special meaning. She explained it to us. Preparing the tea, offering it to a guest and drinking of tea thus served has become the most sophisticated ritual, the highest level of hospitality in Japan. This is the symbolic meaning attributed by the culture to a seemingly ordinary process. In the absence of the accompanying sentiment, it is a mere act of drinking of tea. That one could buy even in a dirty little roadside tea stall in India.

My rational distaste for the symbols ebbed away. On the contrary, I began to experience that symbols serve a useful purpose. Those symbols remained same as before; only my ability to experience the meaning was developing.

I have installed an idol of Lord Krishna in my basement. I started placing a flower at its feet every day. That idol of Lord Krishna symbolically represented the universe, the Truth. The flower represented me. I wished to transcend my ego and to dissolve in the universe. That was the meaning of my symbol-based worship.

Last night, we had a power failure.
Lights went out everywhere.
I stepped out of the house.
Darkness, huge as a mountain, stood in front of me.
In it, I saw Lord Krishna[22]*!*
He revealed himself in the form of infinite darkness.
He was present everywhere; He permeated everything.

This morning, I sat down to practise Dhyana.
In front of me was a little, dark idol of Lord Krishna,
Full of beauty, full of love.
He was playing the flute.

---

22. *Krishna is a dark-skinned god. The word 'Krishna' literally means dark.*

Light streaked through the window.

The dark image bathed in the light!

He had shed away his cosmic identity.

He had become a tiny idol for me.

He was near me. He was in front of me. Enclosed in my eyes.

Lord Krishna made himself visible to me.

The same Lord Krishna,

yesterday, and today.

there and here,

Of the size of the universe, and as small as the idol.

Abstract as well as concrete.

Everywhere, and near me,

and also inside me!

*****

5. Swadharma[23]

(Mission)

23. *The original word used by the author is swadharma -- pronounced as sva-dharma. This Sanskrit term literally means one's own dharma. The term 'dharma' has several shades of meaning, including diverse notions such as the psychological inclination or nature, aptitude, duty, mission, assigned work, chosen work and so forth. The translator, therefore, believes that it would be best to use the original Sanskrit term rather than any one single English word, which would not fully cover all aspects of 'swadharma'.*

For revealing, Truth becomes soul.
For prayer, Truth becomes God.
For conduct, Truth becomes
'Dharma'. (ethics)

— Vinoba Bhave
('Ishavasya Vritti) [24]

24. *Vinoba Bhave's commentaries on Ishavasya Upanishad.*

5.1

During the course of my efforts for spiritual seeking, I sensed that my drive and motivation for daily work grew weak. Now and then I wondered, "Should I retire from regular work so as to pursue the path of spirituality?" How should one combine spiritual seeking and the motivation for daily work? While this question was important for my personal life, it became even more crucial in view of my responsibilities and commitments related to social work. Several questions began to trouble me. If I continued the path of spirituality, would the enthusiasm for my daily duties eventually vanish? Should I or should I not engage myself in the practice of spiritual seeking? Should I disengage myself from my work as a physician and a social worker? What is my *swadharma?*

I came across a statement made by Vinoba -- "The thought that the *karmayoga* (path of action) impedes *dhyana* is incomplete and it needs to be amended. After disengaging from all the worldly duties one can attain the state of trance by the path of *dhyana*. But it should be possible to attain a similar or an even deeper state of trance when one is engaged in discharging one's worldly duties. *Karmayoga* based on physical labour and non-acquisition will be equivalent to meditation. Whatever is generated, created or achieved via physical labour should be respectfully dedicated to the entire society. *The very act of dedication turns anything into spiritual – regardless of whether it is an activity or meditation. Spiritual life does not mean renunciation or abandonment of one's duties, it means reducing your attachment."*

I had been reading *Ishavasya Upanishad* every morning. It gave very clear direction -- One should aspire to live a fully active life of 100 years! One should desire to be engaged in action, performing duties for a hundred years! An idler has no right to live! You will live for 100 years if you perform your dutiful actions.

I found answers, not to just one, but two questions. I found a key to a long healthy life and my question regarding renunciation was also answered. But in what kind of activities should I be engaged?

In the *Bhagavad Gita* it is stated that one should recognise one's *swadharma* and direct all the activities towards fulfilment of one's *swadharma.* In his 'discourses on the *Bhagavad Gita'* Vinoba had said, *"Swadharma* is given to you naturally. No one needs to search for *swadharma.* We did not simply fall out of the sky and started walking around on this earth.... To serve the society in which you are born is a *dharma* you have naturally received. Your *swadharma* is born with your birth. One might even say that your *swadharma* is waiting for you to be born. It is the purpose of your birth, the mission for which you are born. You are born for the fulfilment of your *swadharma."* (Appendix 2).

When I was in the medical school, I harboured a nagging feeling that I was in the wrong place. I had several other interests -- music, literature, social work and so forth. Study of medicine did not hold my single-minded attention and I could not bring myself to be thoroughly engrossed in it. I did not know what exactly I should do. (To say it in today's parlance, I did not know what career I should choose). I was confused and disturbed.

Fortunately, Vinoba was alive and accessible at that time. I went to see him one day and asked him, "I do not understand what my *swadharma* is. How should one look for *swadharma?"*

My question brought a smile to Vinoba's face. He said, "You do not have to hold a lamp and go out in the dark looking for *swadharma.* If you have to go out looking for it, there is something fundamentally wrong. Your *swadharma* is already there, awaiting you; you just do not see it. You do not recognise it because you are stubbornly trying to discover it. Open your eyes and you will see it."

I was not able to see or recognise my *swadharma* at that time. To be really honest, I did not understand what Vinoba said to me at that time. I thought that I ought to choose *swadharma* on the basis of what I like to do and what I do best, as if this was an aptitude test. I considered my liking as the main criterion. And Vinoba pointed out to me how illusive that is. It is a misconception that you are the whole and sole arbiter of your own life and *swadharma* is not to be determined under that misconception. I am ordained in my *swadharma* by my natural inclinations (given to me) and my duty to the society in which I was born and brought up. All I need to do is to let go of my ego-based insistence and recognise and accept what I was born to do. We refuse to accept this simple fact and waste our entire life chasing something else altogether. That is what Vinoba was asking me to open my eyes to.

5.2

At the Johns Hopkins University in the USA, I had learnt a little bit of management science along with the courses related to public health. I was impressed by management philosophy and management techniques. Today the American management science has spread its influence all over the world. It emphasizes a system of incentives in order to motivate human beings to work. Higher profits, higher wages, promotions, status and fame often serve as powerful incentives. Individuals will walk an extra mile in the hope of benefiting from these incentives. If they work more for the sake of personal benefit, the whole society will benefit and that is well and good. Economist Adam Smith, who is regarded as the father of modern capitalism, professed that people are motivated by their self-interest to work hard and that creates wealth and enriches the society.

But there is something fundamentally wrong with Smith's philosophy which I began to realise from my experience. These incentives incite in people's mind an intense desire for financial gains and excessive greed. One could say that the power of incentives lies in their ability to incite such desires and greed. Desire and greed compel a man to work hard. But greed, once aroused, is insatiable and desire knows no limits. Oscar Wilde was right when he said, “There are only two tragedies in life -- one, not to get what you want and the other, to get it!” Under a management system based on a scheme of incentives a man remains deeply unhappy and unsatisfied even after working extra hard.

Leo Tolstoy has written a beautiful story ‘*How Much Land Does A Man Need*?’ which I remember reading in my childhood. At that time it was only an entertaining story; now I understand the piercing truth contained in that story.

Pakhom was a hardworking and enterprising farmer. When he learned that very fertile land could be bought cheaply in the next province, he sold his own farmland and went to that province. He bought the land there and busied himself in cultivation. Soon he was able to sell this new land and buy an even larger farm in another place. Repeating this a few more times, he became fairly rich.

Soon he heard from travellers about a far off country where aborigines lived and the land was very fertile. The travellers told Pakhom that the aborigines did not know how valuable such a land could be to someone. Pakhom began to dream about limitless land to cultivate. His wife said, “We have everything. We have enough. Why do you want to chase after yet more land?” Pakhom said angrily, “You have to put up with inconvenience if you want to progress.” Pakhom left his wife and children, gathered a lot of money and gold, and set off in search of this limitless wealth.

Pakhom reached the land of the aborigines. Just as the travellers had told him, there was unlimited fertile land there. Pakhom was so impatient that he could not sleep well that night. He got up very early the next morning. The aborigines and their chieftain had already gathered. Pakhom offered the chieftain a bag of thousand gold coins and asked for the land. The chieftain agreed with a smile, but said, “Whatever land you can walk around and enclose from sunrise to sunset will be yours.” Pakhom was overjoyed, but kept quiet. He did not want the aborigines and their chieftain to know what big fortune they were giving away! The chieftain continued to explain the rule fully, “If by the sunset you do not reach the same point from which you started at sunrise and you fail to complete the enclosure, you will get no land and your gold coins will not be returned either.” Pakhom made a note of the risk in his mind.

As soon as the sun appeared on the horizon, Pakhom took off and started walking eastward. He walked briskly. He paid no attention to the birds chirping around. His mind was busy figuring out how wealthy he was going to be.

By 10 o’clock, Pakhom stopped to drink water. He ate a little. He had covered quite a distance eastward from the starting point. Now he turned left, i.e. northward. He picked up the pace and walked quite far by 2 o’clock in the afternoon. He brushed aside the thought of eating lunch because he did not want to waste any time. He kept walking. He wondered whether he should turn left again. But the land under his feet was very fertile. He wanted to walk a little more and encompass some more land to the north. The land seemed to call out to him! He did not notice how late it already was.

Pakhom remembered that he must encompass the land from all four sides in order to own it. He turned left and started walking westward. He increases his speed. He was almost running now. To unburden, he dropped the bags of food and water. He cast away the jacket he was wearing. Pakhom watched the progress of the sun across the sky and kept running. He was dripping with sweat.

Soon it was evening. Pakhom turned southward. Now he was trying to complete the fourth side of his traverse. An enormous land was going to be all his. But the sun had almost reached the horizon. Pakhom’s feet were tired. His chest was rising and falling rapidly and he could feel sharp pangs of pain in his breast. He reminded himself of his wife and children. He focussed his mind on the glorious farm he was going to own. He summoned up all the strength that was left in him and then some more and started his last dash. All the people were watching the sun. Will Pakhom complete his traverse?

Pakhom gritted his teeth and ran the final distance. He reached the starting point just as the sun touched the horizon. A wild cheer rose from every aborigine. They knew of no one who had won this much land. They danced with joy.

Pakhom lay still on the ground. The aborigines fell silent. Their chieftain approached Pakhom and said, "All this land is now yours". But Pakhom was dead. Pakhom had died of exhaustion.

The aborigines dug a pit long enough to bury Pakhom. They lowered his body in the pit and covered it with soil. The chieftain looked at the six foot long piece of earth and commented sadly, "He really needed only this much land!"

We are all Pakhoms. And even if we do not start that way, the society turns us into one. The land each one of us covets is different. Some covet money, some desire status, and still others strive for fame. That land gives us a run of our life. If the Pakhoms do not run, who will grab these lands? Therefore we must lust after a land. That is the principle of management! The driving force of greed is necessary to make everyone work hard!

Is it really necessary? Do we not have any alternative but to become Pakhom? Should man's destiny be such a grievous tragedy?

For me this was not a mere philosophical question. It was a question of my life and death. Driven by the work-impulse that the modern world had instilled in me, I had turned even my social work into a field of desire. I had run breathless so that I could do more social work. I had shed away all other facets of life because they had become burdensome. I had raced to cross the finish line ahead of everyone else and almost reached the line of death! The difference between Pakhom and I was that Pakhom died and I survived. But I did not wish to become Pakhom again.

This was a difficult problem. People in the modern world work themselves to death in order to fulfil their selfish desires. Take away the carrots of incentives, these carrots, and the motivation for work is gone! That is why socialism failed. But the temptation of personal gains does not bring happiness, no matter how hard one works.

Ego (power, fame, respect), selfishness (money, wealth, comforts), greed and competition are like four horses yoked to the chariot of today's economic order and these horses are allowed to run wild. These mental drives will leave the rider of the chariot forever unhappy, dissatisfied, groaning with suffering. Like a Greek tragedy, the destiny of modern man is pain and suffering on the psychological level and heart disease on the physical level!

What is the solution? If not greed, then what other motivation can there be for people to work? This is the most intractable question facing the modern world.

***

While reading *Ishavasya Upanishad*, I paused at the familiar lines-- "One should aim to live an active life of 100 years, fully engaged in useful work. This alone is open to you and there is no other way. Actions do not become bondage to a man, (the desire for the fruit of actions does)".

And suddenly came the answer. "The solution is *'Nishkama'*[25] management!" Surely there is a need for management; but not the kind that fans the fire of greed. What is needed is a management that motivates people to work and yet remain free from personal aspirations and ambitions. What is needed is an economic order that does not whip up greed and selfish motives. This is what can be called '*nishkama* management'. Mankind will have to develop the art and science of *nishkama* management. Is *nishkama* management possible? Is *nishkama* management feasible? Will *nishkama* management be effective and beneficial to both the individual and the society?

I have not found satisfactory answers to these questions as yet. Gandhiji spoke of 'trusteeship' as a way to put the principle of *nishkama* management into practice. What did he mean by it? "Think of yourself as a trustee of your body, your talent, your skills,

---

25. *Nishkama -- Pronounced as 'nish-kam(uh)'. This Sanskrit term means 'devoid of desire' for personal gain. (kama = desire, nishkama = without desire).*

your profession and your wealth. As a trustee, you are responsible for taking a good care of these, it is a responsibility placed on your shoulders by nature herself. As a trustee, you are not the owner and you do not have the right to do with these assets what you will. So you ought to use these and carry out all the transactions in this world the way a highly conscientious trustee would." Translating this notion of trusteeship into practice could turn out to be the key to *nishkama* management. Greed ultimately leads to suffering like Pakhom's. But there must not be a withdrawal from action. Can one turn himself into a trustee of his own life, rather than an owner and user?

How to be engaged in the affairs of this world without becoming stressed? *Ishavasya Upanishad* tells us, "Renounce this world in His name and enjoy what you receive". Give away the attachment to the fruit of one's actions and then enjoy what one receives. This is the key. This attachment is like a scorpion's sting. Once you remove the sting, you would come to no harm even if the scorpion crawled all over your body! The poison is not in our actions, it is in our attachment to the fruit of our actions.

So renounce this attachment in His name and enjoy what you receive! Alright! But even when I agree with this commandment, how do I bring my attitude in accordance with it? It is a giant leap for me!

I am yet to find a way to correct this attachment. The mind adheres to old habits and will not let go. Attachment to the fruit of my actions has been its lifelong habit. And people all around me and people everywhere else are similarly 'conditioned' by this same habit. How will a change in attitude come around? How to remove the scorpion's sting?

There seems to be a method to teach the mind. Just as we can slowly train our body to bend and flex by practising yogic exercises every day, we need to train our mind to let go of the sense of attachment by engaging ourselves each day in some activity from which no personal gain or profit is expected. We need to practice the art of renunciation each day. Will I become a little more *nishkama* in this manner?

5.3

After studying the scientific reports of a few select research studies (see Appendix 1) that have made large contributions to the present-day understanding of heart disease, I became more keenly aware that the two scriptures the *Bhagavad Gita* and *Ishavasya Upanishad* and the path on which I was trying to walk are 'scientific'.

Professional work can lead to stress and that stress can lead to heart disease. But from where and how does the stress come about? The scientists found that overwork was not the cause of stress. The stress was due to responsibility, lack of time and the lack of adequate help at work. The scientists found that control and freedom were even more important factors. Those who were in positions of control and had autonomy to make decisions about their own work and working conditions had a relatively mild form of stress while those whose work was determined by someone else suffered a far higher level of stress. Two well-known studies in the USA – the *National Health Examination Survey* and *Health and Nutrition Survey* -- showed that heart attacks were four times more likely amongst those who were overstressed at work compared to the rest of the population.

Once the factors most directly responsible for causing stress at work were understood, it was realised that work per se was not harmful, but the expectations of personal gains from working spawns the burden of responsibility and time deadlines. Work without an attachment or expectation of personal gains would be relatively stress-free.

Dependence, to be controlled by others, generates stress at work. In a large industry, large corporation or a large bureaucracy, any person who must work like a cog in a large machinery finds work very stressful due to the loss of freedom. Loss of freedom causes stress and heart disease. Therefore, a worker should enjoy freedom and be empowered to make decisions both in planning and execution of work. Working in such conditions and a helpful environment generates little stress. In other words, the human need for freedom, love and relationships does not vanish even at the workplace.

Work does not kill. However, the workplace environment and the nature of work in a modern society definitely kills!

Scientists Friedman and Rosenman examined the relationship between a person's psychological make-up and heart disease. Their study recognised two personality types that are poles apart. The scientists termed these polar opposites as 'Type A' and 'Type B'. People with 'Type A' personality traits were found to be very highly vulnerable to heart disease. What are the 'Type A' personality traits? --

- Obsessed with the idea of achieving goals that are nebulous.
- A strong psychological need for success, progress in career and social recognition.
- Competitive.
- Persistent sense of hurry.
- One track mind, concentration.
- Hostility and anger.

In short, a modern-day executive!

Next, the researchers found two most dangerous traits of the Type A personality -- hostility and pessimism. How do these traits express themselves? They express themselves in the form of utterances such as "This world is wretched" or "These people are wretched"; in the form of distrust of others; in the form of negative feelings about others; in the form of frequent outbursts of anger and a marked hostility towards everyone. All these are angels of death!

Two researchers named Grossarth and Matticek found that fatal heart attacks are ten times more likely in people who overemphasize logic and intellect and deny their own emotions than in the rest of the population. Moreover, they have higher risk of death from cancer as well.

Clearly, mind and attitudes greatly influence body, especially the heart. Anatomical heart and emotional heart are very intimately linked. Therefore, there is no escape from heart attack without closely examining one's own mind and emotions and cleansing them.

Ornish's study proved that one could change even after developing heart disease. Other studies have proved that the frequency of heart disease can be reduced amongst the Type A people by changes in personality. Now, are not yoga and pursuit of spirituality a means of cleansing the mind and changing the personality?

The overall effect of Ornish's therapy was remarkably positive because it includes several elements such as a change in diet, physical exercise, cessation of smoking, *shavasana,* relaxation techniques, *dhyana* and change in personality, persons getting in touch with their own emotions and bond to each other in small groups.

Western researchers have discovered several factors responsible for heart disease. Some are internal to the person, others are external and societal. Should each factor be treated separately in a piecemeal fashion? A separate pill, a different medicine and a different treatment for each risk factor? What is needed is not this piecemeal approach, but a holistic treatment, a different philosophy of life, a different lifestyle, a different social organisation. Regardless of whether you adopt the Gandhian philosophy of living or you subscribe to Ornish's therapy; the bottom line is that you need a holistic living that emphasizes natural diet, physical exercise and labour, detachment from the desires and bonding with other human beings by way of love and duty.

5.4

I found Ornish's message "Change your lifestyle to escape from the peril of heart disease" very convincing and it proved very useful to me. Fortunately, educated people in urban settings are beginning to develop a liking, though in a fairly small measure, for a change in lifestyle. Some highly motivated individuals are indeed changing their diet; they are taking an active interest in exercise, yogic postures, and *dhyana*. And since all this meshes very well with cultural traditions of India, many Indians are drawn to it relatively easily even though many find it hard to actually practise it on a regular basis. Is this the answer to heart disease and the disease producing lifestyles? When the entire society is perverse, can lonely individuals live a healthy lifestyle like islands within an ocean? I began to wonder about this.

For the sake of my health, I must avoid sweets, fatty products and fried foods. When I go to someone's house or office, tea is invariably offered. It does contain sugar and cream and is often accompanied by biscuits that are sweet. If you travel in India by train, you face a barrage of soft drinks. In shops, new varieties of processed food appear every day. In old days desserts that used to take a lot of time to prepare at home were prepared only on special occasions. But now, you can buy these in the shops any time you feel like it, and the only effort you need to make is to open their containers. If you go to a restaurant, you do not have to do even that much. And now-a-days you do not even need to go to a restaurant. There is a home delivery system. All you have to do is pick up the phone and call. The arms of the food processing industry have now reached inside the households.

Since large Indian and foreign corporations, motivated by the potential for immense profits, have entered the arena of processed food, new eating habits are being popularised with the use of promotional techniques, commercial jingles and discount coupons. *"Meri jan Meri jan khana murgi ke ande!"* In anticipation of a huge market for processed foods in India, the Government of India decided to permit foreign corporations to enter that market. Was it realised that this decision would bring us heart disease and hundreds of thousands of fatalities in its wake? Even more ironic is the fact that in order to get rich, we buy the stock of these very companies and thus own a piece of our own death!

I remember reading about an amazing snake. The legend has it that when hungry, this snake begins to swallow its own tail and thus literally eats itself! Our relationship with this processed food industry is similar to that snake. We are the shareholders, we are the producers, we are the salesmen, we are the customers and we are the victims too!

In the age of this food industry, in the age of market economy and in the midst of the hedonistic civilisation, how am I or anyone else going to resist temptations and stick to a healthy diet?

Why do these advertisements sing praise of foods that are harmful to health? To intensify people's desire for comfort and pleasure so that they will be more indulgent. Why should people be more indulgent? So that more goods can be sold to them and larger profits can be made. And we buy shares of these companies. Why? Because we want to share the profits. Why? Because we want to get rich fast. Why do we want to get rich fast? Because someone else is already rich and we do not want to lose in the race for the riches! And we sincerely believe that without a race, without a competition, men will not feel motivated to work; without greed, men will not compete and without competition there is no progress.

There is a fallacy somewhere. Once you get stuck in this whirlpool, you do not have time to stop and think. Like that dog in Acharya Rajaneesh's story, everyone is running the race towards death in order to stay alive.

But why do we have to win race? What goal do we wish to reach? And once we arrive there, what do we wish to do next? When a Thoreau or a Gandhi steps aside from this mad race and asks us these questions, what answer do we have?

A folklore similar to this one can be found in many cultures. An industrialist from Mumbai came to the forest of Gadchiroli on a vacation. He saw an aborigine sleeping under a tree on the banks of a stream in the forest. The industrialist shook him up and said,

"Get up! Do not just lie there like a lazy bum!"

"And what shall I do then?"

"Get to work!"

"What will work do for me?"

"You will earn money!"

"And what will money do for me?"

"You can invest that money and make a huge profit!"

"And what will the profit do for me?"

"You will be rich!"

"And what will the riches do for me?"

"You can buy a car!"

"And what will a car do for me?"

"You can take some time off from work and go into a forest like me to relax."

"But that is what I am already doing!"

"..................?"

The original questions remain with us. If wealth in the modern world is derived by exciting people's greed, selfishness, competition and a desire for sensual pleasures and success, is this kind of wealth likely to make man happy?

When you live in a society that constantly excites these desires, how can one individual live a natural, stress-free and spiritual life?

5.5

"There is enough on this earth for everybody's need, but not enough for everybody's greed."

— *Mahatma Gandhi*

Diminishing my desire and greed and turning away from unnecessary 'wants' are crucial to my spiritual development. But the individual spiritual goals must translate into societal goals. The social order that incites desires and greed must be transformed into one that promotes a healthy lifestyle and cultivates pure minds. These societal goals are an inseparable component of the individual spiritual goal.

How could an individual's pursuit of spirituality remain aloof from the responsibility of cultivating spiritual values in the society? The treatment recommended by Ornish is silent about this societal aspect.

Here is where I think Gandhiji outshines all others. He adopted for the purification of life 11 'commandments' distilled from the Hindu texts and added some in the modern context. We recite them in our evening prayers at Shodhgram. The prayer says: "With an attitude of humility and firm resolve shall I observe the principles of non-violence, truth, *brahmacharya* and physical labour; I shall not steal, I shall not acquire and accumulate anything in excess of my need, I shall refrain from succumbing to the pleasure of tongue, I shall be fearless, I shall deem all religions as equal, I shall use what is grown or made in my own neighbourhood and I will not treat anybody untouchable."

But each of these commandments is extremely difficult to follow. The society I live in must be such that there will be few or no impediments to the observance of these commandments. How can the commandment, "Refrain from acquiring and accumulating in excess of my need", compete against the message with which the society persistently barrages me -- "Earn More and Buy More"? Our social norms and messages are diametrically opposite to the glorious teachings of *Ishavasya Upanishad.*

Ishavasya Upanishad tells us, "With a sense of detachment; enjoy what you have received; do not covet anyone else's wealth."

The society tells us, "Earn more; be greedy and desire more, be jealous about others' wealth and strive to acquire it for yourself."

Ishavasya Upanishad tells us, "Aspire to live an active life of 100 years, fully engaged in work."

The society tells us, "As far as possible, shirk physical labour and seek a life of leisure and pleasure."

Ishavasya Upanishad tells us, "Man's deeds are not the bondage. It is the desire for the fruit of one's actions that become a bondage."

The society tells us, "Actions are to be performed for the exclusive purpose for obtaining more and more personal gains. The stronger the desire for fruit, the stronger will be the drive to work. So add fuel to the fire of one's desire".

Our social conditioning evokes a behaviour that is exactly opposite to the teachings of *Ishavasya Upanishad.* If *Ishavasya Upanishad* is correct, then it is irrefutable that today's social values would not make a man happy. What should be the values of the society in which I live and how should that society function if I do not wish to die of heart disease? I began to see this very clearly.

I should not be eating anything that is sugary, fried or rich in fats or animal products. I should not consume foods made from refined flour, I should stay away from foods devoid of fibre. And that means I ought to avoid white bread, biscuits, chocolates, ice cream, butter, cheese, *samosas* and *puris*. (And also animal products like meat, chicken, eggs which anyway I do not eat). And the food industries (dairies, bakeries, food processing plants and restaurants) must change their product lines. Their products must deliver fewer calories, contain less sugar, less cholesterol and higher amounts of fibre. The advertisement businesses ought to change the emphasis of their advertisements and promote health rather than make the food industry's current products appear highly desirable to consumers.

Tobacco products and alcohol are sold at every street corner and have also entered every household via television advertisements and sponsorship of sports. This ought to be changed. Vehicles like cars and scooters and public conveniences like elevators and escalators discourage me from walking, and tempt me away from exercise, while entertainment from television promotes sedentary habits. These habits too ought to be changed.

The messages that encourage excessive consumption of goods and services ought to be changed; the messages that induce people to buy, buy and buy, and messages that emphasize leisure over useful activities ought to be changed. The society pressures people to earn more, to acquire and accumulate more, to blindly chase wealth, power, fame, status, praise, respect and promotion and even to act against one's better judgement in order to gain such things. The society not only conditions and encourages people to act in this fashion, but it also does not hesitate to punish those who would not fall in line. All this is destructive for me.

Poverty causes hunger and malnutrition. If a poor woman is under-nourished, children born to her are low birth-weight babies. Nearly 35% of all the babies born in India have a low birth-weight; they weigh less than two and a half kilograms (five and a half pounds) at birth. Compared to the normal birth-weight babies, the babies with a low birth-weight are several times more likely to suffer from diabetes and heart diseases in adulthood. Thus poverty, malnutrition and under-nourishment of mothers-to-be lead to high incidence of heart diseases. These things ought to change.

A selfish, lonely person, a person cut off from contact with others dies from heart disease. Since relationship with others is necessary for a healthy life, the so-called 'free economy' that breeds competition and selfishness and severs the relationship based on affection and care for others must be considered as a life-destroying force. What is conducive to a healthy life is not the extreme individualism, but the teaching that unites them in a fellowship of affection, respect, human concern and love for each other -- "Aum! Let us protect each other. Let us eat together. Let us act as one." We do not need to build around each one of us the cage of selfishness and loneliness, even though it has been given such pretty names like individual freedom and free economy.

We need free human beings, not free economy!

***

On completing one year after my heart attack, in May of 1996, I wrote to a few of my close friends about my bout with heart disease and my experiences during recovery. The intention was to alert them, so that they may not repeat the errors I made in life and not suffer the way I did. Some of them were in media, they published my letter in newspapers. The magnitude of public response was completely unexpected. As if I had touched a painful chord of the society. Several friends and hundreds of readers wrote to me that my letter served to alert them about the errors of their own lifestyles. Some people who were suffering from heart disease wrote, "I read the story of my own heart disease in your letter." Many asked for my advice regarding the treatment they were receiving. Two very senior and well-known physicians wrote to me, "I have kept your letter in the place of worship at home. Your letter has now become a part of my daily worship."

I saw that my experience of heart disease and its treatment was useful to other people. Many are sick as I was, many are headed the same way I was. They are my fellow patients. I asked myself, "What is the best way to help my fellow patients? What will turn my fellow sufferers into my fellow travellers and fellow seekers?"

The calamity that struck me three years ago is not a mere personal experience any more. It is growing into a global tragedy. Incidence of heart disease, diabetes and high blood pressure have reached an epidemic proportion in India now. The Indian society will have to face the onslaught of these health problems and learn how to treat them and, even more importantly, how to avoid them. The lifestyle will have to be reformed and it will become necessary to learn, accept and live a lifestyle that eliminates the causes of heart disease, reduces the stressfulness of daily living and harmonises social relationships with the environment. In the 21st century, this is going to be the main challenge for the health services and the health industry. In Shodhgram we have made a beginning; we are slowly learning to live such a lifestyle. While we continued our work of medical care to tribals, and research on providing health care to rural population, we also started searching a way to live a healthy and happy life.

The *Bhagavad Gita* begins with words, "*Dharm kshetre kurukshetre*", a spiritual field and a field of duty.

For me, these two fields, my work and the pursuit of spirituality became one and the same.

*****

6. Peace

We must never cease from exploration;
and the end of all our exploring
will be to arrive where we started
and know the place for the first time.

— T. S. Eliot
(Four Quartets)

6.1

Why am I narrating my psychological and spiritual journey? I feel that without it, the story of what caused my heart disease and how I came out of it will not be complete. Without regaining both the meaning of life and the joy of living, my heart would not have healed. Without those two things, I would have been forced to live with a patched-up heart and an ever unhappy mind. Merely a healthy heart muscle was not enough for me. My complete heart; my heart the physical muscle and my heart the psychological entity, in fact the entire living, breathing, feeling person that I am, had to be healed to become one healthy and whole entity. My practice of yoga, *dhyana* and devotion, and the somewhat nebulous understanding of Truth and God, I gained along this journey are indivisible from my heart and the joy of living. My sadness had stemmed from the fact that I was cut off from the universe, I was myself a torn personality and lay shattered in pieces. I was in deep agony. Pursuit of spirituality offered me a vision of the universal presence of the principle called God and that, howsoever, fleeting, experience made my life whole. It relieved my stress, my hankering and my pain. It healed my wounds. It restored my joy. And along the way my heart was healed.

It is been three years now since I was given the new lease of life. How am I doing today?

- I am physically fit. I weigh 58 kilograms; my blood cholesterol level is 149 milligrams, and the HDL level is 47 milligrams.

The ratio of cholesterol to HDL is approximately 3:1, which is considered safe. The blood sugar is well under control. I can jog and ride a bicycle without any distress whatsoever. Dr. R. D. Lele, a very eminent physician and the National Professor of Medicine, invited me to Mumbai and put me through the stress thallium test. The results of that test showed that my heart was normal and the coronary arteries were free of obstruction.

- I am doing all the work and seeing through all my responsibilities as earlier, but I feel a lot less stressed. I am far less anxious to make something happen; my yearning to reach somewhere in life is considerably reduced.

- I am at peace. The uneasiness is substantially reduced. I am trying to live only in this moment.

- My journey along the path of yoga and spirituality continues. I am still ploughing the field of my mind. It has not rained so far, but this act of ploughing is in itself a beautiful experience. I have not reached anywhere, do not know where I will reach, nor do I know if I ever will. And in fact, I do not know if there is any place one is supposed to reach on this path. Maybe there is no destination apart from the process of journey.

There is hope in my life. How joyful and complete is life! And there is yet much to be lived, lot to be discovered.

Out of the 13 resolutions I had made while I lay in hospital bed on May 13, 1995, I have either fulfilled or have done my best to fulfil 12. The only resolution about which I have not been able to do anything is to learn music. And that is because I have not found anyone in Gadchiroli to teach me music. I had a strong desire to go in the Himalayas. Finally, I managed to go. I could walk 20 km in a day and reach up to 12,000 feet high Kedarnath. The unparalleled majesty of Himalayas and the limitless expanses filled me with amazement and humility. Now I know why seekers and sages went to Himalayas.

There are some more things I want to do in life. I want to climb my inner Himalayas. I want to learn music and Sanskrit. I would like to do the physical labour of farming and organically grow enough grain and vegetables for my family. I want to be able to do many such things. After my bout with heart disease, many new ideas about providing health care to new-born babies in village, new research projects to reduce child mortality have been taking shape in our work. But now I no longer feel the compulsive eagerness or stressfulness. Once you know the rhythm of life and learn to dance with it, your steps are not out of sync.

What is my daily schedule?

I get up around five in the morning. I read spiritual books for about half an hour and then take a 40-minute walk. My walk in the forest is one of the high points of my day. On returning from my walk, and a bath, I practice *yogic* postures and *shavasana.* The next half an hour is spent in *pranayama* and *dhyana.* The body and mind try to become one and seek attunement with the cosmic principle. Sometimes I feel it happen and sometimes I feel like I am chasing a mirage; but it is an extremely enjoyable experience nonetheless. My daily work begins around 9 in the morning. After lunch at noon, I spend half an hour on nap and *shavasana.* I end my work at 6 pm. After that we engage in a community prayer session at Shodhgram. At night I spend some time with my children after dinner and then read for about an hour to hour and a half. I once again do *shavasana* and by 10 pm I am asleep.

6.2

I have come to the end of the narration of my journey. But what about the question that begun this journey in the first place? When I felt an acute pain in the chest on April 18, 1995, I was overwhelmed by the fear of death. What about that fear of death? Have I overcome that fear?

The sudden appearance of the risk of death had shaken me to the core. But was it indeed the fear of death? It was not the fear of the moment of death or the fear of death itself. I had been there and back. On the angioplasty table, when the death was imminent, I had understood that death was only dissolution of one atomic arrangement. There was no pain in it. There was no suffering in it. So what was I afraid of?

It was not the fear of death. Death is a temporary event, life is longer! I was afraid of losing the life because of death. I loved life. I wanted to live some more. There was a whole lot of living to do. I was sad because all that was going to slip out of my hands. That is why I had felt unsafe and afraid. Why be ashamed of that?

Now I do not sense that fear or lack of safety. I deliberately chose to say 'I do not sense it'. I cannot be sure that the sense of fear or the insecurity is not lurking somewhere in my mind unknown to me. But I feel I am at peace. Will my mind be at peace when the moment of death comes again? The greatest minds fall prey to fear at that moment. How will I fare?

In *'Mangal Prabhat'* Gandhiji writes about *abhay*[26], "All fear is because of this body. If we could lose our sense of attachment to this body, we would be fearless." About *aparigraha*[27] he writes, "Our

---

26. *Abhay -- In Sanskrit 'Abhay' means 'no fear' (fearless).*

27. *Aparigraha -- In Sanskrit, literally, non-acquisition and non-accumulation.*

body is also one kind of acquisition. Out of our wanton desire for the pleasures of flesh, we sustain this body. Once our desires for sensual pleasure and enjoyment become very weak, we no longer need the body... The entire universe is filled with the soul. Why should the soul then confine itself to the cage of a human body? And why should one engage in all kinds of shenanigans just to maintain this cage?"

I have not reached such an exalted level of spiritual development Gandhiji had, and therefore, when bullets pierced his chest, he was able to chant "*Hey Ram!*"[28]. How will I behave? Will I be able to remind myself, "The day which we fear as our last is but the birthday of our eternity"?

This remains a curiosity. In *Lancet*, the world-renowned medical journal, one often finds interviews of celebrated medical scientists. One of the questions that an interviewer asks was "How do you wish to die?" Most of the interviewees answer that they wish to die in sleep or of a sudden and fatal heart attack. But one scientist had answered that he wished to die while he was fully alert and awake; he wished to witness every moment before death and the moment of death. He did not want to miss that great experience!

Dr. Anil Awchat, a very good friend of mine, whose doctor wife, Sunanda, has been valiantly fighting cancer for last eight years once wrote to me, "Encounter with death is the most searing and purifying experience. Everything unholy burns to ashes in it."

There is a legend of Saint Eknath --

Someone went to Saint Eknath and said, "We are ordinary folks. Our mind is always occupied with thoughts of worldly affairs and with unholy thoughts. How do the saints like you remain free of such thoughts?" Saint Eknath said to him, "Stop thinking about the saints,

---

28. *To die with the Lord's name on the lips is a Hindu ideal. 'Ram naam', name of Rama, was considered by Gandhiji far more powerful than the mythological figure of Rama himself.*

because I can clearly see that you are going to die in just seven days." A great personage like Saint Eknath could not be wrong! That man went home and tidied up his affairs. He said good byes to his friends. He begged the enemies to forgive him. He gave away what he could to charities. On the seventh day, Saint Eknath went to see him at home. The man lay in bed, waiting for the death to knock on his door. When he saw Saint Eknath, he said, "Sir, I will be gone by the end of this day." Saint Eknath asked him, "In last seven days how many times did unholy thoughts cross your mind?" The man said, "What unholy thoughts? All I could think of was my certain death in seven days!" Saint Eknath said, "We saints see imminent death all the time, therefore we can stay free of unholy thoughts and free of sins."

I can give my best wishes to all. Everyone should face death at least once!

6.3

"What should we do now?" On returning to Nagpur on the 20th of May 1995 after my angioplasty in Lucknow, Rani and I started thinking about what we should do in future. We ought to be psychologically prepared for the possibility that I may suffer a major heart attack any time in future. Lack of medical help in the forest of Gadchiroli meant that chances of my survival would be very slim. Should we then continue to live and work there? Or should we settle in a big city where modern medical facilities are readily available? My life would be more secure there, but we would have to abandon the life and work we had embraced until now. What should we do?

I did not want to die. But was it worthwhile to live long if the price was to forgo the goal of life itself? Why should I choose to die today out of fear of physical death sometime in future? We made up our mind to spend the rest of our life there in the district of Gadchiroli. There was no sentiment of 'sacrifice' in this. It was a straight forward decision. We knew that if we had to give up the pursuit of the goal of our lives, life would be meaningless and unbearable to us. *Ishavasya Upanishad* said very clearly -- "Wish for a meaningfully active life of a hundred years. For an embodied soul, this is the only path. There is no path other than this!" I had no other choice. I could at least desire to live for a hundred years pursuing my own mission!

During the month of April 1995, Rani and I had to suddenly go away from Shodhgram for my medical treatment. We were away from Shodhgram for nearly a month and a half. There was no guarantee that I would return alive and well. During those days, all the team members of our small organisation, 'SEARCH' worked with an amazing motivation and sense of unity. No one jumped the sinking ship. All the work continued just as smoothly as before. How vain I had been, labouring under the illusion that unless I did something myself, it would not be done! How false was my belief that I had to be there for anything to be accomplished! Rani has limitless enthusiasm and an exemplary get up and go work ethic. After my return to Shodhgram, we chalked out a new three-year research project to develop a new method of providing medical care to new-born babies born in the homes and huts in villages. If we could develop this solution, may be, it could help saving nearly five million new-born babies who die every year in developing countries. A mission, *swadharma*, was already awaiting me. I was back at work.

6.4

I still do the same old work. Rural and tribal health care and allied research, training village women to become barefoot neo-natologists, patient care at our hospital for tribals, de-addiction, training of youth in rural areas -- all the work of SEARCH is going on smoothly... There is an old adage in the Zen sect –

"Before enlightenment, I used to chop wood and fetch water.
After the enlightenment, I chop wood and fetch water."

I am far, far away from enlightenment. I do the same work I used to do before, but my inner understanding and my attitude has slightly changed. Though fully active, I feel less entangled in the web of our activities. Sometimes I feel angry and sometimes my expectations are not met. Many times my mind gets side-tracked into wishful thinking and dreaming. It often develops irrational attachment to work and its results. But as soon as the mind wanders into the territory of aspirations and expectations, I sense dissatisfaction and stress gaining ground. I wake up, recover my balance, and throw away the unnecessary burden. That always brings more joy to life.

In fact, I have begun to understand how futile it is to force oneself into stubborn bull-headedness. If we learn to float effortlessly in the stream of life, we automatically reach. Try swimming adamantly against the blow of life and you suffocate as the water enters your nose and mouth. But the stream of life has no signs boards that could inform us about its direction and speed. If you do nothing and simply learn to easily float in this stream, you can understand what this stream is all about, where it is taking you and how. I slowly began to realise this simple truth. The Zen masters have said it beautifully —

Sitting quietly
doing nothing
Spring comes and
grass grows
By itself.

The confusion in my mind about the fear of death, about the purpose of my life and about how I should live my life was over. My intellect saw the answer, but I would not say I have understood the answer. It is one thing to know New Delhi on the map but to actually reach there is a different thing. Intellectually I am convinced that this universe, the cosmic Truth behind it and I are one and the same. But, has the ingrained habit of seeing myself as someone different from this universe really gone? To be continuously conscious of what is understood intellectually, to sustain it in attitude and to follow in daily practice is a very long and arduous journey. I repeatedly experience how much this flesh and mind are made up of clay. The reason runs a thousand miles ahead, while the body and the mind slowly crawl forward. They revert to old habits again and again. But the heart does not lose hope. In this striving, in this journey, I experience plenty of joy.

Perhaps I will not be able to go the full distance in this lifetime. There is no assurance that my body will last till then. But, if each day, each moment, became a destination in itself, there will no longer be a need to reach anywhere else. I am progressing at the speed of a tortoise. I am not a hare. I do not have that pace. Nor will I gain that kind of pace. But that does not worry me. The tortoise is crawling. It is still crawling.

My journey continues. Many times I get trapped in the web of illusions -- sometimes due to the circumstances and sometimes of my own doing. But in a few days I see the light and I am free from it. Who can tell whether I am going round and round like a pair of oxen turning a millstone or whether I am on a spiral staircase, arriving at a slightly higher level at the end of each circular lap? And even if I reach the same spot from where I started, I arrive there to find a new understanding, a new realisation.

I still cannot bring myself to see God everywhere and in each one around me. I cannot become one with all the people with total love.

I know that love bonds people, but my reason falls short of that feat. My ego is still there, it has not vanished, nor does it seem likely to vanish. It butts in again and again and becomes an obstruction. But I am improving. I relish the joy of changing myself a little bit each day; I relish the joy of sculpting myself a little bit each day.

I always remember what Jesse Jackson, a Black priest, had said back in 1984 —

"Friends, forgive me for my shortcomings.
God has not yet finished working on me."

*****

7. Some Information and Techniques for Health

Contents : Chapter 7

7.1

Diagnosis of Heart Disease

Heart disease can manifest in several ways -

1. **Sudden Death** The heart suddenly stops beating.
2. **Angina** One or more of the three major blood vessels that supply blood to the heart, develop internal narrowing or block resulting in insufficient blood supply to various parts of heart. There is no discomfort at rest. But while walking or physically exerting, a sensation of pressure or diffuse pain is felt in the vicinity of the heart – in the chest, in the left arm or both arms, in the neck, in the jaw or in the chin. The pain subsides after a few minutes of rest.
3. **Heart Attack** A sudden blockage of a vessel supplying blood to the heart completely cuts off the blood supply to a portion of the heart and that portion becomes permanently damaged. The person feels acute pain in the chest lasting for more than half an hour. Chest pain is often accompanied by sweating, vomiting and exhaustion. Often, chest pains can also arise due to other causes such as extreme anxiety, pain in chest muscles or due to hyperacidity and gas in stomach. Such pain can mimic a heart pain. Conversely, sometimes, no pain accompanies an onset of a heart attack (silent infarction). This can be very deceiving to both the patient and the physician.

4.	**Weakening of the Pumping Action of Heart**	Feeling breathlessness during physical labour or while lying in bed. Swelling of feet.
5.	**Irregularity of Heart Beats**	Palpitation, pulse beats irregularly or very rapidly.
6.	**Heart Block**	Sudden slowing of the heart rate (down to 30 to 40 beats per minute), resulting in dizziness, unconsciousness.

***

7.2

Fats: Which and How much?

1. Fats are made up of fatty acids. A human body needs only 14 grams of fats a day in order to meet the need for fatty acids.

   An American as well as a well-to-do Indian consumes, on an average, 60 to 90 grams of fats each day. Thus 25% to 35% of their daily caloric intake consists of calories from fats. It leads to increase in body weight and cholesterol. A healthy person, (i.e. a person who has no heart disease and whose cholesterol count is less than 150 mg.) should limit his/her fat consumption in such a way that the calories derived from fats are less than 20% of the total daily caloric intake. This means that a normal, healthy, sedentary person should limit his/her daily fat intake to 40 grams or less.

   Those who wish to follow Ornish's method, either for the treatment of a heart disease or for reducing the cholesterol level, should ensure that no more than 10% of their total caloric intake is fat-derived. This translates into daily fat consumption of no more than 20 grams. 20 grams are equivalent to only 4 teaspoons of cooking oil.*

2. **Types of fat** : Just as the amount of fat consumption is an important consideration, it is also important to know which types of fat should be used and which forms should be avoided –

	Fat Type	Foods in which it is naturally present
A	**Saturated fats**	Milk, butter, ghee, red meat, eggs and coconut oil. Saturated fats are also present in some proportion in all other cooking oils.

B	1.	**Unsaturated Fats Mono-unsaturated fats**	Peanut oil (*falli*), sesame seed oil, (*til*) mustard oil (*Saraso or Rai*), olive oil and fish.
	2.	**Poly-unsaturated fats**	Safflower oil, sunflower seed oil and soyabean oil.
		Omega-6	• When consumed excessively, these promote weight gain, reduce body's ability to fight infections and promote heart disease as well as growth of cancer cells. Safflower oil (e.g. Saffola) sunflower oil, soyabeen oil, corn oil have a high proportion of Omega-6.
		Omega-3	• Good for the heart — occurs naturally in mustard / rapeseed (*sarso*) oil, fish (though fish also contain saturated fats), to some extent in soyabeen oil, lentils (without removing the seed coverings), beans, and green vegetables. Limit the ratio of Omega-6 to Omega-3 fats to 5:1.

*The views on dietary fat intake vastly differ. While the Ornish diet recommends very low fat, some others recommend liberal use of unsaturated fat and restrict the carbohydrate intake (the so called Low-Carb or Keto diet). It is prudent to avoid the extremes.

3. Cooking Oils

- All oils are 100% fats, very rich in calories. So the oil intake needs to be carefully controlled.
- Except for the coconut oil and palm oil, all cooking oils and foods derived from vegetables primarily contain unsaturated

fats. But all these oils also contain, to a lesser degree, saturated fats as well. And vegetable oils too promote weight gain.

- During frying, the unsaturated fats in cooking oils change into trans-fatty acids, which are suspected of promoting heart diseases and cancer.

4. Dietary Sources of Fats and Proportion (%) of Fatty Acids in Them

No.	Source of Fats	Saturated Fatty Acids (SFA) %	Monounsaturated Fatty Acids (MUFA)%	Polyunsaturated Fatty Acids (PUFA) %
1	Coconut oil	87.9	7.8	0.8
2	Corn oil	12.7	24.6	57.4
3	Cottonseed oil	25.9	22.9	47.8
4	Peanut (groundnut) oil	20.9	47.9	29.9
5	Mustard or Rapeseed oil *(Saraso)*	10.7	56.0*	32.6
6	Sunflower seed oil	9.1	25.1	66.2
7	Olive oil	14.2	71.5	8.2
8	Palm oil	47.9	37.9	9.0
9	Safflower oil *(Karadai oil)*	10.7	17.7	78.5
10	Sesame seed oil *(Til)*	13.4	41.2	44.5
11	Soyabean oil	13.1	28.9	57.2
12	Butter	49.8	20.1	1.8

* Includes 8.9% of Oleic acid and 46.5% of Erucic acid.

(Source.: 'Nutritive Values of Indian Foods' by C. Gopalan, National Institute of Nutrition, Indian Council of Medical Research, Hyderabad, 1994)

It is recommended that the saturated fats in the diet should be eliminated or vigorously reduced, and the amount of Omega-6 fats should be reduced. While keeping the consumption of total fats within the safe limits, the amount of monounsaturated and Omega-3 fats should be increased; they are not conducive to heart disease.

Unfortunately, no oil commonly used in India has ideal proportions (i.e. very low in saturated fats, high in monounsaturated fats and Omega-3 fatty acids). Olive oil, or canola oil are not easily available in India. By mixing in equal amounts the mustard oil, peanut oil and soyabeen oil (all three of which are easily available in India), a proper balance between monounsaturated and polyunsaturated fatty acids (Omega-3 and Omega-6) is achieved. Such a mixture also contains the least amount of saturated fatty acids. PUFA (polyunsaturated fatty acids) in mustard oil contain a high amount of Omega-3 fatty acids, which are good for the heart. On the other hand, advertisements for safflower oil or sunflower oil claim that these are good for the heart; but the PUFA in them include high amounts of Omega-6 and low amounts of Omega-3, and monounsaturated fatty acids, which makes safflower and sunflower oils unsafe for the heart.

In order to increase the content of Omega-3 fatty acids in your diet, it is better to increase the amount of green vegetables, lentils with their seed coverings and beans rather than using oil.

5. **Milk** (The data in the table below pertains to the varieties of milk available in India)

	Type of Milk	**Saturated fats (%)**	**Calories (per 100 millilitres)**	**Calories from the fats (out of total calories)**
1	Buffalo milk	7.0	100	70 %
2	Cow milk	4.0	70	50%
3	Dairy milk	4.0	70	50%
4	Toned milk	3.0	61	45%
5	Low Fat milk	2.0	52	35%

6	Double Toned milk	1.5	47	22%
7	Skimmed milk	0.0	35	0%

Butter = 80% fat, Ghee = 100% fat

Fats in milk, yogurt, butter and ghee are harmful because they are saturated fats. They increase the cholesterol. Low fat milk is better than a full-fat milk. Skimmed milk is the kind of milk that has no fat or cholesterol. Those who are already suffering from heart disease or those who wish to reduce the cholesterol should use skimmed milk even to lighten the tea or coffee. If they wish, they should use yogurt or buttermilk made from the skimmed milk. You can buy skimmed milk powder in a store and make skimmed milk from it at home by adding water. Such skimmed milk costs same as the usual milk from dairy.

6. Eggs and Meats

Eggs and most of the meats contain high levels of fat and those fats tend to be of the saturated variety. Egg yolk and meats are therefore harmful for the heart.

7. How much fat can you consume if you have heart disease?

According to the Ornish method, a patient of heart disease should limit the consumption of fats to 24 grams per day. These should consist of 8 grams each of monounsaturated, polyunsaturated (Omega-6 and Omega-3 in a 5:1 ratio) and the saturated fatty acids.

This can be accomplished by the following measures —

- 20 grams of the three-oil mixture (mustard oil, peanut oil and soyabeen oil) per day. Rest of the fat comes from the 'invisible fat' present in various food items.
- Remember that 20 grams of the three-oil mixture and the fats already present in other food items in a daily meal provide the 8 grams of saturated fats and do not try to deliberately add a source of saturated fat.
- Use whole lentils and green vegetables.

7.3

How to Improve Your Diet and Reduce Your Weight

Common shortcomings in the diet of well-to-do Indians are the following --

1. Inadequate amount of green vegetables, salads and fruits.
2. Use of white flour from which bran has been removed and the polished rice.
3. Low fibre and antioxidants intake due to (1) and (2) points mentioned above.
4. High amount of saturated fats, the main sources being ghee, milk and milk products, eggs and meat.
5. High consumption of sweets and fried foods. Fried foods increase body weight. Moreover, the process of frying generates trans-fatty acids which have been identified as carcinogens.
6. Low proportion of Omega-3 fatty acids.
7. The other common deficiencies are of proteins. Vitamin B12 and Vitamin D, soluble fibre, iron.

I have found the following measures and guidelines very helpful in order to improve diet and to reduce weight --

1. Do not rely on the established tables of 'ideal weight'. Those tables were constructed at a time when body mass index of 25 to 30 was considered safe. Now, there are three yardsticks for determining a healthy weight for you –

   - **Body mass index (BMI)** = $\dfrac{\text{Weight (in kg.)}}{(\text{Height in meters})^2}$

     BMI should be between 18 and 21.

   - Waist/Hip Ratio should be 0.85 or less.

   - You should maintain throughout your life the same weight you had at the age of 25. (Unless you were already overweight at that age.)

These three yardsticks should serve as a guideline for determining what body weight to aim for.

1. 'Eating more and exercising less' causes an imbalance, which increases fat in the body and increases weight. When we consciously change this imbalance, the weight decreases.

2. Reduction in food intake alone helps to decrease the weight, but its effect is short-lived. For permanent decrease in weight it is important to build muscles, which burn more calories and hence decrease body fats. For that, follow a regimen of regular exercise.

3. Thus, in order to regulate weight, we need to regulate how much and what we eat *and* how much we exercise.

4. Walking is an excellent form of exercise. One should walk 3 to 4 kilometres every day. In order to shed excess weight, additional walking will be helpful.

5. One kilogram of fat tissue in human body is equivalent to 8000 calories. If we burn 300 calories a day by exercising, it will take a month to burn away 300 x 30 = 9000 calories; i.e. to reduce the weight by about 1 kilogram (2.2 lb.). This assumes that we do not overeat at the same time.

6. To burn away the body fat:

   - Walk every day.
   - If you walk fast, you can burn more calories per minute. Hence, do not walk at a leisurely pace. Walk briskly. Make your walk an 'aerobic' exercise.
   - Do your household chores that involve physical labour.
   - Work in the garden around your house or on a farm.
   - Stand instead of sitting.

7. Food fats and sugar are the two components that build up fat tissue in our body. Food fats represent 9 calories per

gram. If these are not burned away by way of physical labour, nearly 97% of the fats in consumed food are turned into body fat. Sugar represents 4 calories per gram and contains no proteins, vitamins or fibre. Therefore, calories from sugar are also referred to as 'empty calories'. Refined carbohydrates are quickly converted into sugars in the intestine. Hence, they should be avoided.

8. Since our childhood we are given sweets containing sugar and fat as a reward or to celebrate a happy occasion, so our palate always looks forward to be treated to sweet fats. The liking for these is like a compulsive habit. It generates an intense yearning. One cannot eat too much of just sugar; nor can one enjoy eating simply a fatty substance. But the combination of the two is irresistible and we are tempted to over eat such combinations. In addition, obese people are especially fond of desserts! This is a circle of evil.

9. Edible oils, butter, ghee and cheese visibly contain fats. In addition, milk, milk products, desserts, chocolates, candies, ice cream, eggs, meat, fried foods and products made from peanuts (peanut butter, for instance) are also high in fats.

10. First, decide how much total edible oil all the members in the family should consume in a month. The person responsible for grocery shopping should buy only that much quantity. Use a mixture of peanut oil, soyabean oil and mustard oil. The person in the kitchen should use the quota of edible oils on a weekly basis from the monthly stock.

11. The limits specified for fats are not for young children. Since they are in the growth and development stage, their calorie needs relative to their body weight tend to be higher. However, remember that the eating habits formed in childhood stay with them throughout their life; therefore, it is the responsibility of adults in the family to not overindulge the children with sweets and fats.

12. Do not consume fried foods or desserts more than once a week.
13. Most processed foods, bakery products and fast foods contain refined carbohydrates and no fibre. Avoid their use as far as possible.
14. Include sprouted lentils in the diet.
15. Start every meal with sprouted lentils, salad, carrots, cucumbers, soup or butter milk etc. Serve the main course only after these are eaten. That limits the consumption of the main course and you can 'diet' without going hungry.
16. Our digestive system breaks down the consumed food and converts it into sugar. If we consume all our daily food in only two large meals a day, it generates a 'sugar flood' twice a day inter-phased with long periods of low sugar levels caused by the excessive insulin secreted in response to the 'sugar floods'. If, however, we eat smaller portions 4 or 5 times a day the body will not experience big swings -- periods of high and low levels -- of sugar. A human body was not designed for eating two stomach-full of meals a day. Our ancestors roamed in the jungles all day and fed all day as and when they found food in small quantities. If we spread our recommended daily intake of food over four or five sessions it is in harmony with how we have evolved to be. Not surprisingly, it also reduces the blood cholesterol level.[29]
17. It goes without saying that increasing the frequency of eating sessions must not result in eating more of total quantity. Each meal should include a small portion.
18. Do not eat any sweets between the meals. Blood sugar shoots up as soon as you consume a sweet. Because of the insulin secreted in body, in response to the increased blood sugar, the sugar level rapidly decreases in about 2 hours.

---

29. *Intermittent fasting – an approach recommended by some to control weight and reverse diabetes, advise the opposite.*

However, the insulin continues to act for 6 hours, leading to low blood sugar (rebound hypoglycaemia) tempting you to eat some more sweets again. Thus, sweet demands more sweet.

19. Instead, if you are really hungry between two meals, snack on sprouted lentils, carrots, roasted beans (*chana*) with their skin, tomatoes, cucumbers and butter-milk made from skimmed milk.

20. We often tend to eat as a relief from stress and anxiety. Even if we are not hungry, the mind desires to eat something. To distinguish real hunger from these false and psychological ones is a part of re-educating oneself. Moreover, find the right ways to reduce the levels of stress and anxiety.

21. Do not remove the bran from flour (do not use maida), the reddish skin on grains of rice, skin on the lentils and do not peel potatoes. Do not use polished rice -- polishing removes fibre from rice. Use brown bread (i.e. bread made from flour that has retained the bran).

22. When fruits are squeezed to extract the juice, the fibre is left out. When you drink that juice, you consume simple sugar in the fruit and that creates a flood of sugar in your blood. It is far better to eat the fruit than to drink fruit juices.

23. Before a meal, eat two spoonfuls of fenugreek *(methi)* seeds either as sprouts or as a powder. It is high in fibre content, and hence, reduces the sugar flood and cholesterol. Some people, however, may suffer from excess gas generation because of fenugreek. They should start with half spoonful before each meal and gradually increase the intake.

24. To reduce the use of oil in cooking, use Teflon-coated utensils.

25. Regularly measure your weight, body mass index, waist/hip ratio, blood sugar and cholesterol. Keep a record in a file or diary. This helps you know your current levels, decide goals and measure the progress.

7.4

A-swad: Mahatma Gandhi

(*A-swad* means refraining from the temptations of taste and flavour. It was included in the 11 observances [vrata] to be followed in the ashram of Mahatma Gandhi.)

"...... Food has to be taken as we take medicine, that is, without thinking whether it is tasty or otherwise, and only in quantities limited to the needs of the body...... . It is therefore a breach of this observance to take anything just for its pleasant taste. It is equally a breach to take too much of what one finds to one's taste. .... it would be sheer hypocrisy to add any other thing to our food, deluding ourselves that it is necessary for the body if as a matter of fact it is not."

"Thinking along these lines we find we have to give up many things that we have been enjoying, as they are not needed for nutrition. And one who thus gives up a multitude of eatables will acquire self-control in the natural course of things. His many desires will become quiet....... This subject has received such scant attention that choice of food with this observance in view has become very difficult."

"Parents, out of false affection, give their children a variety of foods, ruin their constitution, and make them slaves of the uncontrolled desire of the palate. When they grow up, they have diseased bodies and perverted tastes. The evil consequences of this early indulgence dog us at every step; instead of controlling our body and senses we waste much money and fall an easy prey to the medicine man."

"No one need take fright at my observations, or give up the effort in despair. The taking of a vow does not mean that we are able to observe it completely from the very beginning; it does mean constant and honest effort in thought, work and deed with a view to its fulfilment. We must not be thinking of food all the 24 hours of the day. The only thing needful is perpetual vigilance, which will help us to find out very soon when we eat for self-indulgence, and when in order only to sustain the body. This being discovered, we must resolutely set our faces against mere indulgence."

— *Mahatma Gandhi*
in '*Mangal Prabhat*'

7.5

Fibre

In 1975, when I was studying at the Postgraduate Institute of Medicine in Chandigarh, the world-renowned surgeon Dr. Dennis Burkitt visited the institute. He was known for his research work in Africa where he had discovered a new form of cancer (Burkitt's Lymphoma). At the beginning of his lecture, he showed us one slide, which made the audience of doctors first grimace and then laugh. The slide showed faeces of two men, one Black African and one White European. The stool of the Black African seemed copious in amount and spread out on the ground because of soft consistency. In comparison, the stool of the White man appeared like pebbles -- hard and dry.

Burkitt explained how these two forms of stool represented two different cultures. The diet of the African Blacks (and of the rural Indians) consists of plenty of grain, lentils, roots and vegetables; so their stools were copious, soft and moist. They defecated twice a day. The diet of the White people (or the modern urban population) had considerably changed. So their stools became hard, shrunken and dry. They could manage even if they defecated only once in a couple of days. And since the stools are dry, they could clean themselves up with paper.

What changes in diet did the modern urban lifestyle bring?

With modern lifestyle the proportion of white flour (without bran), sugar, fats, animal proteins and milk in the diet increased and the amount of fibre decreased. Why was the fibre important? Enzymes in the human intestine do not break down fibre, so it remains intact and unabsorbed in the intestine. In the end, it gets expelled in the stool. Since fibre absorbs and retains water, it causes stool to swell and remain soft. In addition, the cholesterol is trapped within the mesh of fibres and gets expelled along with the fibre in the stool. As the amount of fibre decreased in the diet of modern man, the stool became hard and dry; and the toilet paper became prevalent in bathrooms.

If the only question accompanying the changed stool was whether to use water or paper for cleaning after a bowel movement, no further discussion would have been necessary. However, Burkitt attributed a whole new group of diseases to the shortage of fibre in diet. This group of diseases is similar to today's Syndrome X. According to Dr. Burkitt, in cultures wherein the diet is low in fibre and stools are hard, the following diseases are highly prevalent -- heart disease, obesity, diabetes, gall stones, hernia, appendicitis, piles, varicose veins and colon cancer.

To avoid these diseases brought about by the dietary habits of modern culture, Burkitt advised us to increase the amount of fibre in the diet, and thereby, to soften and increase the volume of stools.

Elderly, traditional people in India worry a lot about constipation. When they describe at length the minute observations of their stool, we physicians think of it as a neurosis. We laugh at their anxiety about the consistency of stool. But Dr. Burkitt presented a scientific basis for such seemingly exaggerated anxiety about stool. At one place Vinoba has written, "*Prabhate mal-darshanam*". Every morning watch your stool carefully. It is a mirror of your health. (See Chapter 2, page 74).

7.6

Benefits of Exercise

"A generation ago, most people needed rest after the day's hard work; now it is the opposite!"

1. Prevents diseases and helps better control if they are already present.
   - Heart disease, high blood pressure, obesity, diabetes.
   - Blood sugar, blood pressure and the harmful LDL cholesterol decrease, beneficial HDL increases.
2. Reduces the risk of death.
3. Reduces stress and anxiety; makes the mood cheerful.
4. Exercise becomes a pleasurable activity.

Figure 2 given below shows the relationship between physical fitness and death rates. The first bar represents a group of people who did not exercise. The middle bar represents the group of people who exercised moderately and the last bar represents the people who exercised heavily. The height of each bar stands for the number of deaths per 10,000 people in a year. Two inferences can be drawn from this graph: (1) the death rate amongst those who exercised was nearly half that amongst those who did not exercise; and (2) moderate exercise was as effective as the hard exercise as far as reducing the death rate is concerned.

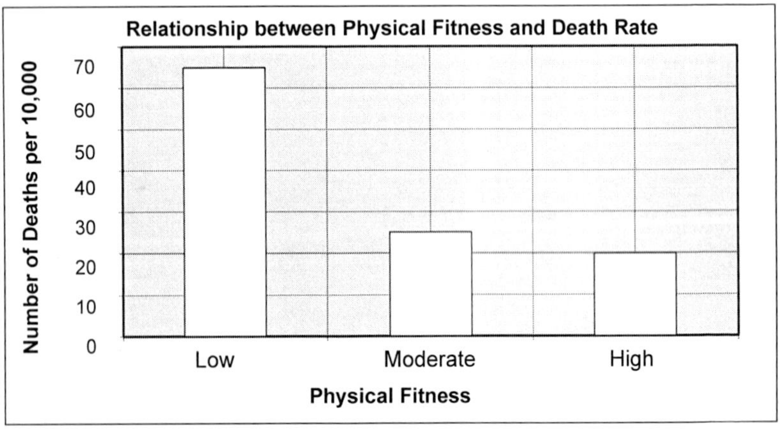

Source: S. N. Blair et al.; 'Physical Fitness and All Causes of Mortality', JAMA (1989), 262 (17): 2395-2401

(Figure 2)

7.7

How Fit are You Physically?

Heart rate (pulse) is a good indicator of physical fitness. Learn to identify the radial artery on the front side of the wrist, two inches above the wrist line and towards the outer side (side of the thumb.) Feel the pulse by pressing on this artery lightly with the tip of the index and the middle finger of the other hand. (See Figure 3 below). Learn to locate it and feel and count its beating. Count the pulse for ten seconds. When multiplied by six, you get the pulse rate per minute. This is the rate at which your heart beats.

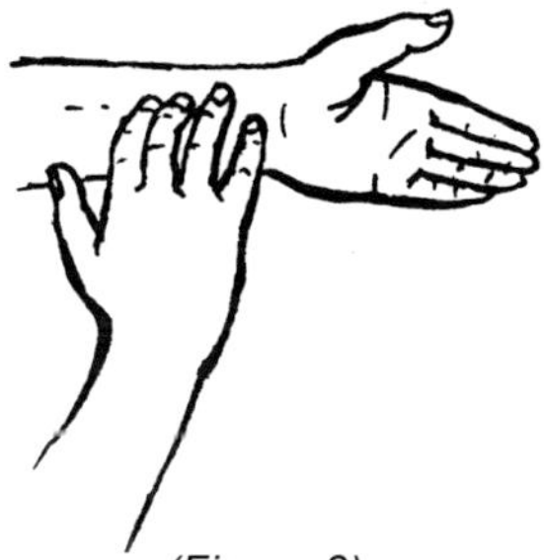

(Figure 3)

Measuring Your Fitness - Method No. 1

Count your pulse after resting for ten minutes. The slower the pulse, the more fit you are (But if it is slower than 50 or faster than 100 per minute, see your physician). The table below gives an idea of how fit you are from your resting pulse rate.

	Age (years)	Physically Unfit	Moderately Fit	Excellent Fitness
Men	20 - 29	86 and faster	60 - 85	Less than 60
	30 - 39	86 and faster	64 - 85	Less than 64
	40 - 49	90 and faster	66 - 89	Less than 66
	50 and over	90 and faster	68 - 89	Less than 68
Women	20 - 29	96 and faster	72 - 95	Less than 72
	30 - 39	98 and faster	72 - 97	Less than 72
	40 - 49	99 and faster	74 - 98	Less than 74
	50 and over	103 and faster	76 - 102	Less than 76

Measuring Your Fitness - Method No. 2

Another indicator of your fitness is the time it takes for your heart rate to return to normal after exercise. (Those with a heart disease and those who feel chest pain and/or feel dizzy while stepping on and off should not take this test). To test yourself, step on and off an 8 inches tall step every 2 seconds (i.e. 30 times a minute) for 3 minutes. Then rest for half a minute and count your pulse. See the table below to get an idea from your pulse rate as to how fit you are.

	Age (years)	**Physically Unfit**	**Moderately Fit**	**Excellent Fitness**
Men	20 - 29	faster than 101	76 - 101	75 or less
	30 - 39	faster than 103	80 - 103	79 or less
	40 - 49	faster than 105	82 - 105	81 or less
	50 and over	faster than 107	84 - 107	83 or less
Women	20 - 29	faster than 111	88 - 111	87 or less
	30 - 39	faster than 113	89 - 113	88 or less
	40 - 49	faster than 115	90 - 115	89 or less
	50 and over	faster than 117	92 - 117	91 or less

7.8

Which Exercise is Right for You?

Varieties of Exercise and Their Effects

Effects of exercise on your body can be grouped into 5 categories -- fitness, stamina, muscle strength, flexibility and balance. Various types of exercise affect the body in various ways. The effect of selected exercises on body are tabulated below:

(* = little, * * = fair, * * * = good, * * * * = very good, * * * * * = excellent)

EXERCISE	Fitness	Stamina	Muscle strength	Flexibility	Balance
Aerobic Exercise	* * * *	* * * *	* * *	* * *	* * * *
Badminton	* * * *	* * *	* * *	* * *	* * * * *
Cricket (Batting)	* *	* *	* * *	* * *	* * *
Cycling Slow (8 km./hr) Fast (19 km./hr)	*** * * * *	* * * * * * * *	* * * * * * *	* * * *	* * * * * *
Dance	* * * *	* * *	* * *	* * * * *	* * * * *
Soccer/Field Hockey	* * * *	* * * *	* * * *	* * *	* * * *
Jogging (8 km./hr)	* * * *	* * *	* * *	* *	* * *
Jogging (14.5 km./hr)	* * * * *	* * * *	* * * *	* *	* * *
Judo/Karate	* *	* * *	* * * *	* * * * *	* * *
Skipping Rope	* * * *	* * *	* * * *	* *	* * *
Swimming (Fast)	* * * *	* * *	* * * *	* * * *	* * * *
Tennis	* * *	* * *	* * * *	* * * *	* * * * *
Walking - Brisk	* * *	* * *	* * *	* *	* *
Walking - Aerobic	* * * *	* * * *	* * * *	* * *	* *
Weight Lifting	*	* * * *	* * * * *	*	* * * *
Yoga-asanas	*	* * *	* *	* * * * *	* * * *

We are looking for an exercise of medium intensity resulting in moderate fitness. To find the hardest exercise is not our goal. Looking at the above table with this in mind, we find that walking, jogging, bicycling, dance, swimming, badminton and yogic exercises would be quite useful. Walking and yogic exercises stand out as two types of exercises that need no equipment and pose no hazards of accident and bodily harm. Their main benefits complement each other. Together, these two exercises offer all the desired effects in good measure. We could also choose dance, swimming or badminton in lieu of these two exercises. Each of these yield all these benefits.

The above table shows that the benefits of walking, jogging and bicycling are more or less similar. Personally, I prefer walking for the following reasons:

1. For the past three million years, i.e. during the evolutionary period in human history, from Lucy up to the most recent past, man, the biped, has walked at work. He had to run only for a short time either during hunting or for saving his life. At all other times, he walked for hours through the forests in search of food. In cattle-raising societies, man walked all day long herding and tending the animals. In agrarian societies, man walked to get to his farm, to fetch water and to gather firewood. Even today, people in villages walk for hours. They have to. Outside of sleeping, man has spent most of his time walking. Thus man has a relationship with walking for the past three million years; walking is man's heritage! No other form of exercise can be construed as a 'heritage'. And that is why, structurally, a human body is designed for walking. In comparison, driving a car or a scooter or sitting in front of the TV to watch a game of cricket are 'exercises' with only a legacy of few decades; the human body has not adapted to these. Maybe it will, after a few million years! But before that several generations will be sacrificed. Especially you and I! If we try to live in opposition to our biological destiny, premature death is guaranteed.
2. Sages of antiquity advised, *"Charaiveti"* "Walk on!" That advice is not only metaphoric, but also literal! Indeed we ought to walk! Death catches up with him who stays put in one place and just sits. If you do not wish to die (prematurely), then move and walk.

3. Walking needs no other equipment except footwear; needs no companion.
4. At the speed of aerobic walking, 8 km (5 miles) per hour, we can gain the same level of fitness that jogging would impart and we would burn calories at the same rate. Though hard to believe, it is a scientific truth. As you increase your pace, the category of walking changes --
    - 4 km per hour = 1 km in 15 minutes = Strolling
    - 6 km per hour = 1 km in 10 minutes = Brisk walking
    - 8 km per hour = 1 km in 7.5 minutes = Aerobic walking

Aerobic walking is a high intensity exercise and it is equivalent to jogging. It also imparts the same level of fitness as jogging does (See Figure 4). Walking faster than the aerobic walking is an unnatural form of exercise, called 'race walking' and it increases the oxygen demand tremendously, even more than jogging.

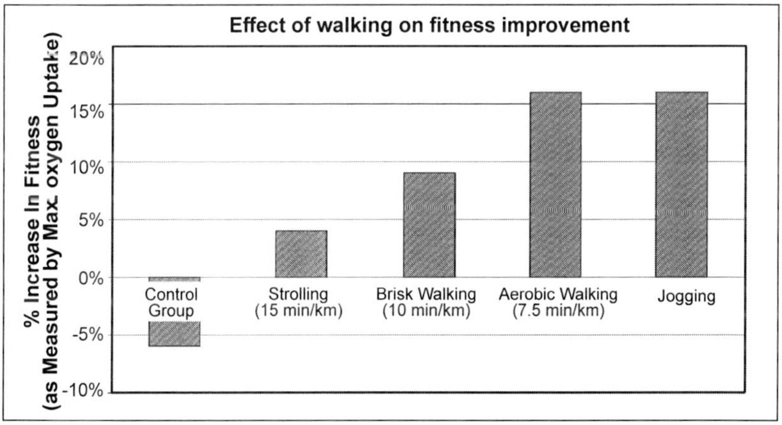

Source: Natural Sport Walking Study Inst. For Aerobic Research, Dallas, Texas

(Figure 4)

The rate of burning calories depends upon the pace of walking (Figure 5). If one walks briskly, one would burn 180 calories in 30 minutes. At the speed of aerobic walking, one would burn 300 calories in 30 minutes, i.e. same number of calories as if one were jogging. I am not recommending that everyone must walk at the pace of aerobic walking. But this information helped me understand the scientific superiority of walking as an exercise.

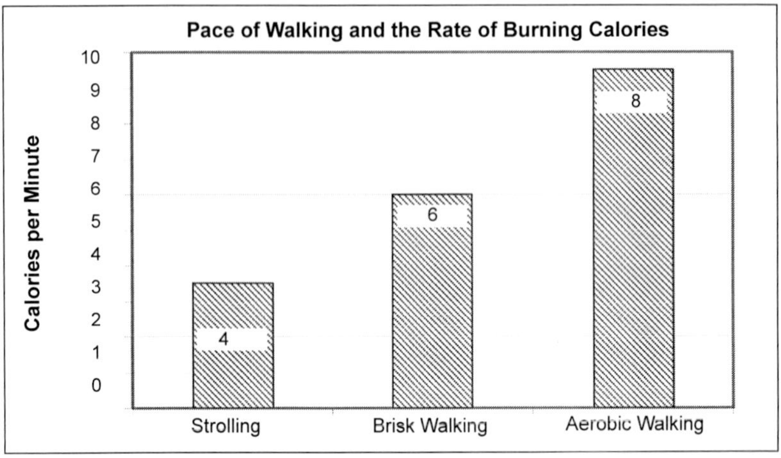

(Figure 5)

5. While walking legs or feet do not get sprained, one does not fall down, one does not get injured or suffer a fracture. I came across a very meaningful statement:

   "Only thing which running can give but walking cannot is injury!"

6. While walking one can enjoy the scenery around, can think, also pay attention to one's breath and keep up with that rhythm. And that is joy galore!

7.9

How Much Exercise?

The Western experts recommend a 30 minute exercise every day or a one-hour exercise three days every week. However, I think this is too mechanical a calculation: 30 x 6 = 60 x 3. We would not advise anyone to sleep or to eat three times a week. These are essential activities to be done daily. When exercise does not remain only a necessity for physical fitness; but becomes a joyful experience, exercising every day is the natural thing. However, if for some reason one skips a day, then the above equation can serve as a guideline to compensate for the missed activity by exercising longer the next few days.

You can set your own limit for the intensity of exercise by counting the heart rate. The upper limit of the intensity of exercise depends upon the capacity of your heart and is not the same for all individuals. You can individualise it by counting heart rate while exercising.

At birth, the maximum heart rate is 220; i.e. heart can beat at the rate of 220 per minute at most. This maximum heart rate decreases at the rate of one beat per year from the time of birth. Therefore,

Your present maximum heart rate = (220 - your present age).

Let's say your current age is 50 years. Then your maximum heart rate at present is 220 - 50 = 170. Consider 170 as 100% of your heart's capacity. The useful effect of exercise (called 'training effect') occurs when your heart beats at 50% to 85% of its maximum capacity. For a 50 year old person, this number will lie between 85 and 142 beats per minute. Once this simple formula is understood, one can calculate the 50% to 85% of the maximum heart rate for himself to exercise appropriately.

When you begin the regimen of daily exercise, initially aim to maintain the heart rate at 50 to 60% of the maximum heart rate determined for your age. In 8 to 12 weeks of such a practice, you can gradually increase the intensity of exercise such that you reach and maintain the heart rate at 80 to 85% of the maximum. Do not hurry, do not over do. Do not hurt your body. Remember that exercise has to become a part of your lifestyle and you need to work slowly at it. When this simple thing is forgotten, people focus on achieving the ultimate goal of 85% of the maximum heart rate and painfully struggle to achieve it as they do with other ambitions. That simply defeats the entire purpose. The exercise may involve some physical effort and straining, but it should be painless, smooth and natural. You do not need one more ambition to seek after. Since the 'training effect' of exercise is experienced when the heart rate can be maintained at more than 50% of the maximum heart rate, you do not have to rush to the 85% goal. If you cannot achieve 85%, even 75% is still good and your body will benefit from it. Do not treat your body like a horse and whip it to make run faster and faster. Instead, coax your body gently with genuine affection and concern.

If you cannot manage counting the heart rate, use a simpler method called the 'Borg Scale'. This scale starts at 6 and goes up to 20. The numerical values are assigned on the basis of your perception of exertion. When you are simply resting, it has a value of 6. The level of exercise that feels like fairly light to you has a numerical value of 11. The 'training effect' begins at this level of exercise. You should try to maintain a level of exercise between 11 and 15, i.e. from 'fairly light' to 'hard'. The heart rate at these levels is usually around 55% and 85% respectively of the maximum heart rate.

BORG SCALE

Rate of Perceived Exertion (how strenuous a physical labour you feel?)

6	
7	Very, very light
8	
9	Very light
10	
=====	=====
11	Fairly light
12	
13	Somewhat hard
14	
15	Hard
=====	=====
16	
17	Very hard
18	
19	Very, very hard
20	

Desired Level of Exercise Is Between These Two Lines (11 - 15)

How much? How fast?

Everyone has to determine for himself or herself the right answer to this question. If the intention of walking is to reduce weight, the faster the better. If the intention of walking is to make the body and the heart physically fit, the pace of walking should maintain the heart rate between 50% and 85% of the maximum heart rate. Figure 6 below shows the heart rates reached during different speeds of walking. One would conclude that a walking pace equivalent to a moderate intensity exercise, i.e. 'brisk walking' is sufficient. We know that it can halve the risk of death (Fig. 2). If reaching the uppermost limit of exercise level (i.e. 85% of maximum possible heart rate) is important for you and it cannot be reached by brisk walking, then you should resort to 'aerobic walking'. As a therapeutic measure or a preventive measure against heart disease, 85% of the maximum possible heart rate offers no additional benefit. Therefore "brisk walking is the best form of walking". (See Chapter 2, page 83) for George Sheehan's recommendation. Remember, 6 km/hour or 4 miles/hour = brisk walking).

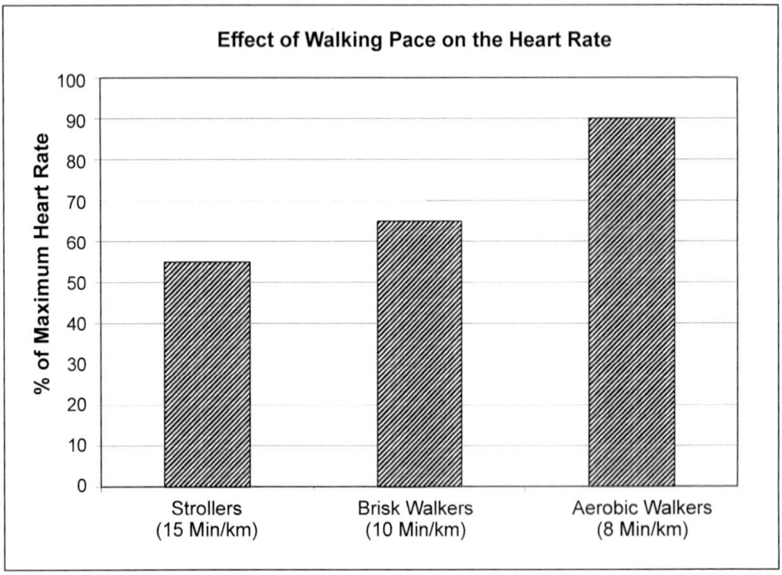

Source : Natural Sport Walking Study.
Institute of Aerobics Research, Dallas, Texas.

(Figure 6)

7.10

How to Walk

1. If you intend to walk for the physical fitness and therefore wish to maintain a certain pace, do use special walking shoes. In the beginning, I believed that was merely the new generation's indulgence and therefore I stubbornly insisted on wearing the Indian style of leather slippers *(Chappal)*.

   But I could not walk fast. And when I tried, I repeatedly ended up with sprains. When I first used the special walking shoes and experienced its ease, comfort and help in gaining the pace, I slapped myself for having been so stubborn. (Rani still refuses to wear the walking shoes. Sometimes she even walks barefoot! She often complains about the feet getting sore and the ankle getting twisted). The walking shoes do not have to be very expensive or have a lot of frills. All that is necessary is they should be comfortable for your feet. High heel shoes, well-cushioned running shoes and sports shoes are unnecessary, and bad for an exercise walk.

   - Shop for walking shoes in the afternoon or evening. Your feet are a little expanded at that time of the day. That is the right time to select the size.
   - The front portion of walking shoes (where your fore-foot fits in) needs to be a little bit flexible. Hold the shoe and try to bend the front half including the sole. It should bend a little. When you walk, and are lifting the leg behind, the heel lifts up first while the fore-foot remains on the ground. At that moment, the shoe needs to bend and not remain stiff like wood.
   - The heel of a shoe needs to be firm. When we walk, our heel is going to land on the ground first. Our body weight will be transmitted to the ground through the heel of the shoe. The heel does not need cushioning. You need

cushioning of the heels when you are running, so that the jolting impacts can be reduced. But that is not necessary when you are walking. For walking, the heel of your shoe ought to be firm, not softly cushioned.

- The heel must not be high. Running shoes, fashion shoes and women's high heel shoes fail miserably when it comes to exercise walking. Heel of walking shoes must not be more than half an inch high.
- When buying shoes, put on both the shoes. Our feet are seldom exactly the same size; one foot is often slightly larger than the other. The shoes ought to fit comfortably on both the feet.
- Briskly walk a few steps on a hard surface. (Not on the carpet! That will only deceive you!) This is the most important test. Your feet must not feel any discomfort when you walk briskly on a hard surface.

(Figure 7)

2. Study the various elements of exercise walking such as posture, planting of feet, swinging of arms etc. and practice them at home. When you begin exercise walking, make sure that every action is correct. Slowly they become ingrained habits and occur without your conscious attention as you walk.
3. Figure 8 shows the correct and wrong posture while walking. Check your posture from the top to the bottom of your body:

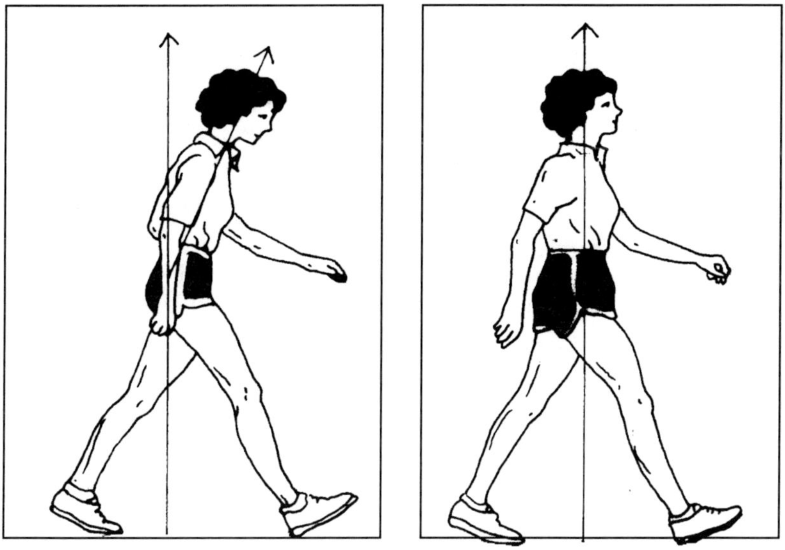

(Figure 8)

- The head should be held up straight; not leaning to one side, nor leaning forward. The chin should be parallel to the ground. To achieve that, do not look at the ground. Look straight towards the horizon. That will keep your head erect (See Figure 8). To watch the road below, just turn the eyes downward; do not bend you head down.
- Keep your shoulders straight, right under the ears. Do not lift your shoulders up while you walk; let them remain loose.
- Keep the back straight and let the chest jut out front.
- Keep the hips right under the shoulders.
- Ears, shoulders and hips should be in a same vertical line landing on the ground at 90^0.
- You will find that not letting the head bend down when you walk is the biggest challenge. When you bend the head down, due to its weight, the shoulders and the back also bend down and spoil the posture.

4. Of what length should your stride be when you walk? A tall person will naturally have a longer stride than a short person. However, that does not affect the pace of walking. Short people (especially women) move their feet faster and compensate for the short stride. If the muscles in the back side of the thigh (hamstrings) are stiff, it is hard to maintain a long stride. That is why stretching exercises before walking are important.

5. During walking, the lower limbs move forward and backward through the hip joint like a pendulum. Let's suppose we are about to plant the right foot forward. (See Figure 9). At that time the leg should not be bent at the knee, it should be absolutely straight. Then, while bringing the left foot forward, the left leg has to be bent at the knee and the foot lifted from the ground. (See Figure 10). Now the entire weight of the body is resting on the right foot. The right leg is straight like a pillar. The left leg now comes forward. It should land on the ground without being bent anywhere (See Figure 11). Now the right leg must be lifted off the ground by bending at the knee and brought forward. But it should be straight and not bent at the knee while landing on the ground. A leg should bend at the knee only when it is being lifted off the ground to move it from back to front. If a leg is bent at the knee while landing the foot on the ground, you trot like a horse instead of walking and your body receives a jolt of lifting up and landing down with each step, like the clowning walk of Groucho Marx.

6. When landing the foot on the ground, let the heel touch the ground first. At that moment, the toe and the sole of the foot should be off the ground so, that the entire foot is making an angle with the plane of the ground. (See Figure 11). This is called the 'heel plant'. In order to accomplish a proper 'heel plant', the entire body and especially the back, the chest, the shoulder and the head have to remain erect and straight. Your purpose is achieved. It is difficult to accomplish a proper heel plant with the head bent down.

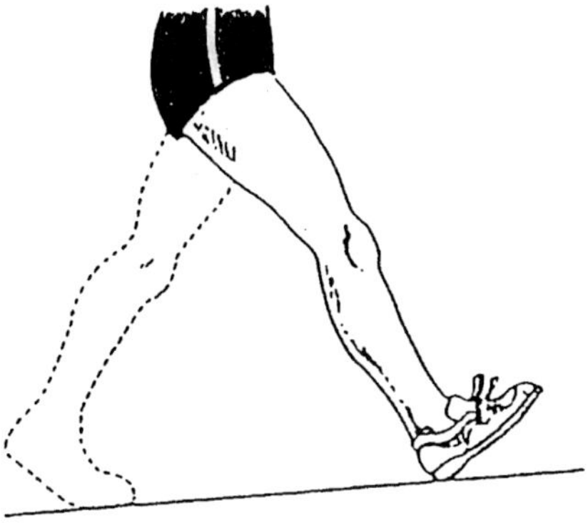

(Figure 9)

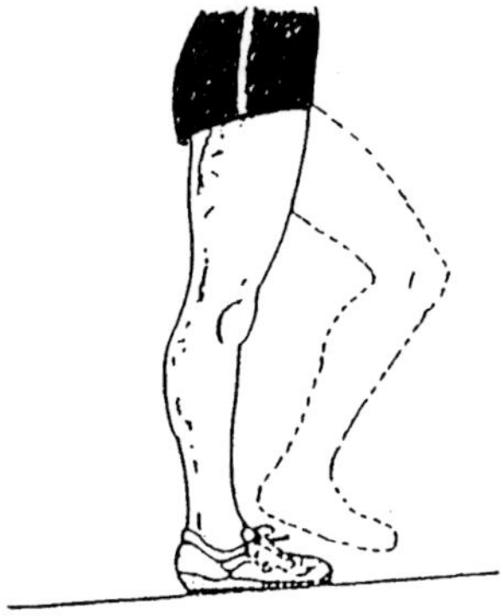

(Figure 10)

7. While landing the foot on the ground, the leg behind which is still in contact with the ground can be used profitably for increasing the pace of your walking. Let's suppose that the left foot is about to land on the ground and we have begun to lift the right foot up; only the right heel is off the ground and the right forefoot is still in full contact with the ground (See Figure 11). At this instant, if you push down on the right forefoot as if to push the ground backward, it will propel the entire body forward, increase the pace and will also exercise the muscles of the calf. In order to generate the power for walking from the muscles of the calf as well as from the hip and thighs, all you need to do is to remember to push the ground backward with the help of the front part of the foot of the trailing leg.

8. Start your exercise walk only after practising the proper posture, stride and heel planting techniques at home.

9. While commencing the walk, do a warm up exercise for two to three minutes and then a few stretching exercises. The stretching exercises should be directed at stretching the muscles of the feet, calves, thighs and the waist. A yogic exercise called *Surya-namaskar* (a highly stylised sequence of postures) is ideally suited for this purpose and only three or four cycles of a

Surya-namaskar are enough to take the body through all the necessary stretching.

This preparation, warming and stretching, prepares muscles for exercise, ensures a proper blood supply to the muscles, increases the length of the stride and makes the joints more flexible. These help avoid fatigue and sprains from walking. The soreness in body often experienced after unaccustomed exertion like walking is prevented or reduced considerable by the warm up and stretching before the exercise.

10. Begin your walking with strolling. The strolling pace is 4 km/ hour. It makes the heart beat at 55 to 60% of the maximum heart rate. During the strolling phase, check your posture and walking technique often and make any needed amendments. For the initial few days to weeks, only stroll.

11. At this stage, pay special attention to the regularity of walking. Make no excuses for not walking. Stay at the strolling pace and gradually increase the distance covered. Note the distance walked each day and increase it finally up to 4 km. per day. Increase your pace only after you have been regularly walking 4 km. each day at the strolling pace. Now try to attain the brisk walking pace (6 km. per hour). First regularity, then the distance and finally the speed. Do not reverse this order by focussing on speed first. For those who are just beginning to engage in exercise walking and for those who have a poor fitness level, Ornish has suggested a timetable as follows:

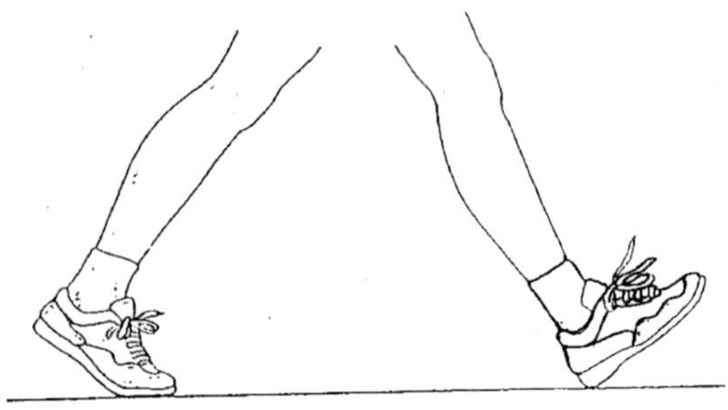

(Figure 11)

Week No.	Duration of Each Walk	How Many Times a Day?	Desired Heart Rate	Borg Scale Value	How Many Days a Week
1	15 minutes	2	50% - 60%	10 - 12	6 - 7
2	20 minutes	2	50% - 60%	10 - 12	6 - 7
3 to 5	30 minutes	1	50% - 70%	10 - 13	6 - 7
6 to 8	40 - 50 minutes	1	60% - 75%	11 - 14	6 - 7
9 to 12	40 - 60 minutes	1	60% - 80%	11 - 15	6 - 7

12. Now the body is accustomed and tuned. Every day, following the initial warm-up, stretching exercises, 5 minutes of strolling and 5 to 10 minutes of brisk walking, the body feels free of tightness in the joints and stiffness in the limbs. The heart rate will have increased up to the target zone. Count your pulse. You are going to continue walking at this pace for 20 more minutes. At the end of those 20 minutes, count your pulse once again and confirm that you indeed maintained the heart rate within the target zone.

13. Then slow down and walk at the strolling pace. This is called 'cooling down'. It has been observed that stopping suddenly after an intensive exercise can lead to arrhythmia (irregular beating of heart) in some people. That is why a cooling down period for slowly easing to a complete stop is recommended.

14. After you come to a complete stop, do the stretching exercise or Surya-namaskar again to nicely relax the muscles.

15. For increasing the longevity, this moderate intensity exercise (i.e. brisk walking) is sufficient. What kind of exercise is good for those who want an additional increase in physical fitness? I observed that during brisk walk my heart rate would increase up to 70% to

72% of the maximum heart rate. I was not able to able to raise it to 80%. So I began to run a short distance. But the sequence of walking and running and again walking and running would not let my mind relax.

16. That is when I learned about aerobic walking. If, while walking briskly, you bend both the arms at the elbow to make a perfect right angle and move them back and forth rapidly as you walk, (See Figures 12 and 13) it automatically speeds up your legs and you find yourself walking at the speed of 8 km. per hour. The heart rate climbs above 80%. This is called 'aerobic walking'. The intensity of exercise is as high as running. It uses up 10 calories per minute, so it is highly useful for weight reduction. Everyone does not need to engage in aerobic walking; nor is aerobic walking necessary for avoiding heart disease or to add a few years to the life. But those who need to reduce weight should consider adding aerobic walking to the walking schedule after 12 weeks. On any day, the aerobic walking should be commenced only after first walking briskly for about 10 minutes. Then, add no more than 5 minutes of aerobic walking. Then gradually increase the duration of aerobic walking to 20 minutes. At the end, slowly decrease the walking pace to brisk walking. (Straighten the arms instead of bending them at the elbow, you will find yourself slowing down from the aerobic walking pace to the brisk walking pace).

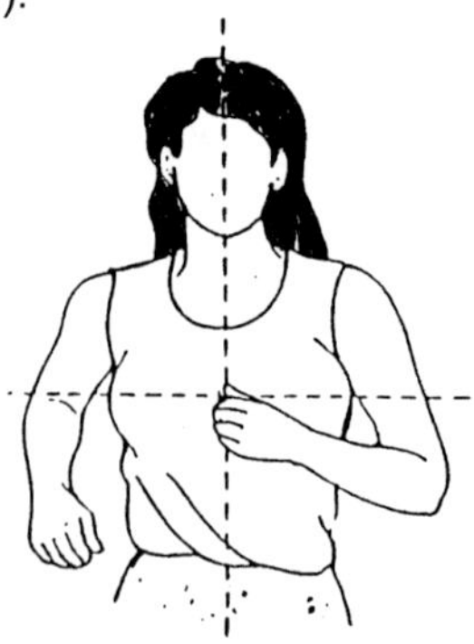

(Figure 12)

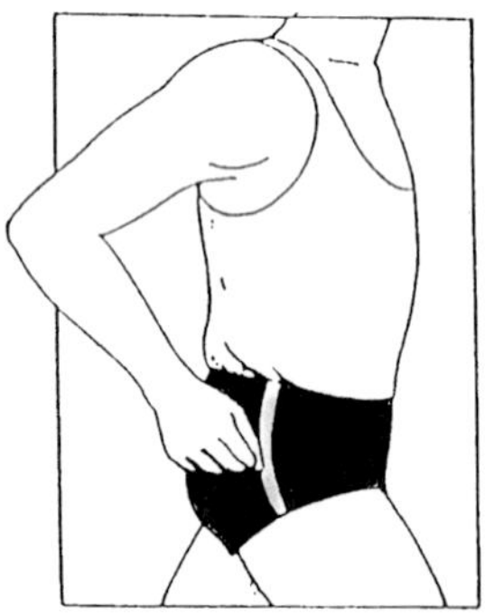

(Figure 13)

After 5 minutes of brisk walking down, slow down to the strolling pace and cool down, stop walking, do the stretching exercises and finally rest.

17. Be mindful of your posture and walking technique. Check frequently from the head to the toes to correct yourself.
18. Keep a daily written record of how far you walked, the time required and the heart rate you attained.
19. Over and above these 18 suggestions, three important points to remember are:
    - Those who have heart disease should set the limits of exercise only after undergoing a treadmill test and consulting a physician.
    - If at any time during walking you feel a pain in the chest or extreme exhaustion, stop and consult a physician.
    - LET WALKING BE A JOYFUL ACTIVITY, not a mere physical chore. Try to attain a rhythm and mental tuning in your walk; let your walking become a sort of *dhyana*!

7.11

Physical Labour: The Spiritual and Moral Angle

Everybody, including me, is experiencing what happens to our body when our life has no physical labour. Why not then do some productive work instead of mere fitness exercises such as walking, running and push-ups?

Vinoba has beautifully explained, "There is a word in Sanskrit for productive work -- *'Udyoga'*. It is a compound word formed by combining two words -- *ut* and *yoga. Ut* means high or noble. *Udyoga* or productive work is the supreme yoga. If man had no hunger and if nature had not endowed man with a motivation to do productive work for satisfying the hunger, man would have destroyed himself."

Bread-labour was an important part of Gandhiji's system of moral values. Gandhiji considered productive work a pursuit of spirituality and believed that whatever is needed for nourishing one's own body should be produced through one's own physical labour. Therefore, everyone who lived in Gandhiji's ashrams had to work in the field or join the work of cleaning or cooking. Gandhiji even put India's national leaders such as Pt Nehru and Sardar Patel to work in his ashram by assigning them the work of cutting vegetables in the kitchen. His thoughts on why physical labour:

"The law, that man must work to live, first came home to me upon reading Leo Tolstoy's writing on bread-labour. But even before that I had begun to pay homage to it after reading John Ruskin's *Unto This Last.* The divine law, that man must earn his bread by labouring with his own hands, was first stressed by a Russian writer named T M. Bondaref. Tolstoy advertised it and gave it wider publicity. In my view, the same principle has been set forth in the third chapter of the *Gita* where we are told, that he who eats without offering sacrifice eats stolen food. Sacrifice here can only mean bread-labour.

Reason too leads us to an identical conclusion. How can a man, who does not do body labour, have the right to eat? 'In the sweat of thy brow shall thou eat thy bread,' says the Bible. A millionaire cannot carry on for long, and will soon get tired of his life, if he rolls in his bed all day long, and is even helped to his food. He, therefore, induces hunger by exercise, and helps himself to the food he eats. If every one, whether rich or poor, has thus to take exercise in some shape or form, why should it not assume the form of productive, i.e. bread-labour? No one asks the cultivator to do breathing exercise or to work his muscles. And more than nine tenths of humanity lives by tilling the soil. How much happier, healthier and more peaceful would the world become, if the remaining tenth followed the example of the overwhelming majority, at least to the extent of labouring enough for their food!"

— Mahatma Gandhi
in 'Mangal Prabhat' (1932)

*****

Appendices and References

Appendix 1

Selected Scientific Studies
on Heart Disease

Appendix 2

Swadharma
(From the 'Talks on the Gita' by Vinoba)

Appendix 1

Selected Scientific Studies on Heart Disease

Studies on heart disease, insulin resistance and 'Syndrome X' in people of Indian origin have been mentioned earlier in this book. Some other important studies are briefly presented below --

1. **Framingham Study:** In 1949 a study was initiated in Framingham, a town 20 miles away from Boston, USA. Back in 1949, Framingham was a town of 24,000 inhabitants. The study aimed to find out the causes of heart disease and who are most likely to develop the disease. A total of 5,209 men and women aged 30 to 62 were selected for this study using the sampling methods. Details of what they ate, what they drank and the minute details of their lifestyle were recorded. They were put through full medical check-ups and this procedure was repeated every two years. This study has been going on for more than 50 years. Out of the original 5,209 subjects in this study many died; many others developed heart disease or other diseases. These illnesses were diagnosed by the attending physicians or came to light during the medical check-ups that took place every two years. The extensive records of innumerable minute details of the 5,209 subjects and their lives yielded invaluable information about who is likely to develop heart disease and why. The study established the relationship between heart disease on one hand and the etiological risk factors outside human control (gender, heredity, age) and the factors within human control (increased cholesterol, lowered

HDL, smoking, obesity, lack of exercise, diabetes and high blood pressure).

The original 5,209 subjects had children during the course of this study. These were also included in the study. The study has now been extended to include the grandchildren also. Participation of three generations in the study is helping the researchers understand the effect of heredity also.

Seven Country Study: But what are the reasons for heart disease outside USA? To find an answer to this question, a seven-country study was initiated during the late 1950s. A total of 12,000 middle-aged people with widely different lifestyles from Finland, Italy, Greece, Japan, Netherlands, Yugoslavia and USA were included in this study. The investigation went on for several decades. Heart disease was found to be most prevalent in Finland and USA, least prevalent in Japan, Italy and Greece. Assuming that the lifestyle of people in the Mediterranean countries (Italy and Greece) must be protecting from heart disease, the investigations were then directed towards finding out the factors in the Mediterranean lifestyle that are protective to heart.

2. **Roseto Study:** A large number of immigrants from Italy have settled in a rural community of Roseto in Pennsylvania, USA. In 1950, these immigrants represented an assemblage of tightly knit family units, adhering to their traditional Italian lifestyle and family relationships. Everyone felt secure in this community. Researchers found that the rate of occurrence of heart disease among the Italians in Roseto was much lower than that among the White Americans in nearby town of Bangor. The following factors seemed to protect the Roseto Italians from heart disease -- (1) use of olive oil and fish in diet, (2) close relationships within families, (3) emphasis on retaining social and cultural traditions brought along from Italy and (4) stress-free living (singing and dancing, lack of

psychological inhibitions and a very relaxing siesta -- nap in the afternoon after lunch).

A researcher named Wolf predicted that in course of time the traditional lifestyle and close-knit family ties of these Italian immigrants will wither away, they will mainstream into the stressfully competitive lifestyle of White Americans and the incidences of heart disease amongst them will rise.

Twenty-five years later, Wolf's predictions came true. Incidence of heart disease in Roseto and Bangor became similar.

3. **Migrant Studies:** Japanese people were found to have much lower rate of heart disease. Was it due to some hereditary factors? Many Japanese have now settled on the islands of Hawaii. Though their genetic heritage is Japanese, their lifestyle has become American. A study of these Japanese immigrants to Hawaii showed that after their lifestyle became fully Americanised, the incidence of heart disease rose to the same level as among the mainland Americans.

   Results of a study conducted by Deepak Bhatnagar and his associates in Punjab, India and in United Kingdom also showed corroborating evidence. Heart disease was relatively rare among the family members who continued to live in rural Punjab at that time. However, it was more prevalent among the members of the same families who migrated to major cities like Chandigarh in Punjab or emigrated to United Kingdom. Migrants to major cities in Punjab or United Kingdom exhibited high prevalence of such risk factors as high cholesterol levels, obesity and increased blood sugar. Incidence of heart disease was found to be more among the Punjabi immigrants than among the White or the Black population of United Kingdom. These Punjabi immigrants had a 'safe' lifestyle when they lived in rural Punjab. But some risk factors in their body seem to express themselves in life-threatening manner regardless of whether they move to major cities in India or to United

Kingdom. The country of residence -- whether India or United Kingdom -- makes no difference. No matter in which country they choose to live, the well-to-do, educated and modern urban lifestyle carries high risk of heart disease.

4. **Alameda Study:** Berkman and Syme studied 4,775 White Americans in the Alameda county of California, USA. After an extensive check-up, the researchers assigned a score on the 'social network index' to each subject on the basis of whether they were married or single, their relationships with other family members, friendships, participation in church activities and social relationships. These people were revisited after 9 years. Death rate among those who had low score on social network index was found to be twice as high as compared to the people with high score on social network index. It goes to show that social bonds protect the heart while selfish attitude and lonely life invite death.

5. **Competitive Monkeys:** A group of laboratory monkeys were maintained on a high-fat diet. It was expected that their cholesterol levels will rise and they will soon be afflicted with heart disease. Out of these monkeys, some were aggressive bullies. These aggressive monkeys were divided into two subgroups. Monkeys in one subgroup were kept in the company of their own type and the other subgroup was kept in the company of quiet, peaceful and non-aggressive monkeys. Observations over a period of 22 months showed that among the aggressive monkeys that lived in the company of other aggressive monkeys (and were therefore constantly exposed to an environment of fierce competition) the rate of heart disease was twice as high as among those aggressive monkeys who lived in the company of non-aggressive monkeys. (The story of a dog told by Acharya Rajaneesh turned out to be quite true)!

*****

Appendix 2

Swadharma

(From the 'Talks on the Gita' by Vinoba)

Arjun used not merely the language of non-violence, but even that of *sannyasa,* complete renunciation. But was this, his *swadharma?* Was this his true nature? Arjun could have cheerfully donned the garb of a *sannyasi,* but how could he have lived the life? If, in the name of *sannyasa,* he went into the forest he would start killing the deer there. Therefore, the Lord told him plainly, "Arjun, your present reluctance to fight is delusion. The nature that has become yours through the years will not permit you to refrain from fighting."

Arjun felt at odds with his *swadharma.* But however unattractive a man's *swadhurma* may be, he has to find fulfilment by persisting in it, because it is only through such persistence that growth is possible. There is no question of pride involved here. This is the law of growth. *Swadharma* is not to be taken up because one thinks it is noble, or given up because it seems lowly. In fact, it is neither great nor small. It is equal to our measure. In the words of the *Gita, "Shreyaan swadharmo vigunah."* (One's own *dharma*, is the best for oneself.) The word *dharma* means not the organised religions, like Hindu *dharma*, or Muslim *dharma,* or Christian *dharma.* Every individual has his own distinct *dharma*. The 200 people who are in front of me have 200 different *dharmas*. Even my own *dharma* today is not what it was 10 years ago; it will not be the same 10 years hence. As the course of one's life changes through thinking and experience, one's old *dharma* drops off and a new *dharma* comes in its place. One achieves nothing by self-willed obstinacy in this matter.

However superior other's *dharma* may appear to be, it is not good for me to adopt it. The light of the sun is dear to me. It helps me grow. The sun claims my worship too. But if, for this reason, I wish to give up living on the earth and, go to the sun, I would be burnt to ashes. On the other hand, even if living on earth is quite dull by comparison, even if the earth is quite despicable when compared with the sun, even if it has to borrow its light – even then, so long as I lack the capacity to stand the sun's blaze, I shall have to stay away from the sun and keep growing on the earth. If someone were to say to a fish, "Milk is costlier than water; come and live in this milk," would it agree? Fish can only live in water; it will die in milk.

Even if someone else's *dharma* seems easier, one should not take it up. Quite often, it only appears easier. If a man in his household life is not able to look after his children properly and, getting disgusted, gives up the world, it will turn out to be hypocrisy and will even become burdensome. At the first opportunity, his old habits and associations will re-assert themselves. When a man goes into the forest because he is unable to bear life's burdens, the first thing he would do there is to build himself a small hut. Then, to protect it, he would put up a fence. Going on thus, he will find that there too he has to manage, if anything, a bigger household. If a man's mind is truly detached, surely renunciation is not difficult for him. There are many texts in the *Smritis* (sacred codes) which show how renunciation can be easy. It is really a question of one's attitude. One's *dharma* consists in following one's true nature. The question is not whether it is high or low, easy or difficult. The growth must be real and fulfilment genuine.

In the Second Chapter in *Gita,* three great truths are declared. First, that the spirit is immortal and indivisible. Secondly, that the body is perishable and transient. Thirdly, that *swadharma* cannot be cast aside. Of these, *swadharma* is in the form of a duty to be performed; the other two have to be known and realised. This *swadharma* comes to us naturally. One does not have to go out in search of one's own *dharma.* It is not as if we have dropped down from the sky and started walking on the earth. Before we were born, our society existed, our parents existed and our neighbours existed. We are born into this stream of existence. To serve the parents who gave me life becomes my duty from birth; so too, the duty of serving the society into which I am born. The truth is that, as we are born our *swadharma* is also born with us. Or we can even say that it is there waiting for us even before we are born; for it is the purpose of our being born. We are born to fulfil it.

Some people say that *swadharma* is like one's wife; just as the bond of marriage is considered indissoluble, the bond of *swadharma* also cannot be broken. But even this comparison does not seem to me to go to the heart of the matter; it is only the second best. I would compare *swadharma* to one's mother. It was not left to me to choose my mother in this birth. It had already been determined for me. No matter what sort of person she is, there is no pushing her away. That is precisely the case with *swadharma* – it is inescapable. Besides *swadharma*, we have nothing else in all this world to rely on, to rest in. To disown one's *swadharma* is to disown oneself, to commit suicide. Only with its help can we move forward. That is why no one should ever let go his shelter of *swadharma*. This is a fundamental principle of life.

Our *swadharma* comes to us with such ease and naturalness that we should cherish it without effort. But because of many kinds of illusion, this does not happen; or else, it is performed with great difficulty; or even if it is practiced, it gets corrupted with many sorts of faults. There are many external forms assumed by the illusion which strews thorns in the path of *swadharma*. Yet, if we examine them, only one thing is at the bottom of it all, namely, a restricted and shallow identification of oneself with the body. Myself, and those related to me through the body, set the limits of my expansion. Anyone outside this circle is to me a stranger or an enemy. This identification with the body builds a wall around me and cuts me off; and the odd thing about it is that I regard only the bodies as "me" and "mine." Falling into this double trap of identification of oneself and one's people with the body, we start putting up all sorts of little walls. Almost everybody is busy doing this. Of these enclosures, one man's is larger, and another's smaller, but after all, each one of them is a wall. And it is no thicker than his skin. One man puts up an enclosure called "attachment to family" and lives in it; another builds and lives in an enclosure called "attachment to nation." One wall divides Brahmins and Non-Brahmins, another divides Hindus and Muslim. In this way, not one or two, but many such walls have been erected. Wherever you turn, you see nothing but walls...as if we could not live without these walls within walls. But what is the result of this? Only one thing: the germs of base thoughts multiply, and the health which is *swadharma* is destroyed.

— ***Vinoba***

*****

Bibliography

1.	Reversing Heart Disease	Dean Ornish	Callantine Book, a division of Random House Inc. New York.
2.	Ishavasya-vritti (Marathi)	Vinoba Bhave	Paramdham Prakashan Paonar, Wardha, 442 111
3.	Talks on the Gita	Vinoba Bhave	Paramdham Prakashan
4.	Maha guhame Pravesh (Hindi)	Vinoba Bhave	Sarva Seva Sangh, Rajghat, Varanasi
5.	Ashtadashi (Marathi)	Vinoba Bhave	Paramdham Prakashan
6.	Vinoba Sahitya (Hindi)	Vinoba Bhave	Paramdham Prakashan
7.	Santancha Prasad (Marathi)	Vinoba Bhave	Paramdham Prakashan
8.	My Experiments with Truth (Autobiography)	Mahatma Gandhi	Navjeevan Prakashan, Ahmedabad
9.	From the Yervada Jail (Mangal Prabhat)	Mahatma Gandhi	Paramdham Prakashan
10.	Hatha Yoga Pradipika – Light on Hatha Yoga	Swami Muktibodhanand Saraswati	Bihar School of Yoga, Munger, Bihar

11.	Light on Yoga	B. K. S. Iyengar	Harper and Collins Publishers, 7/116 Ansari Road, New Delhi – 110 029
12.	Light on Pranayama	B. K. S. Iyengar	Harper and Collins
13.	Light on the Yogasutra of Patanjali	B. K. S. Iyengar	Harper and Collins
14.	Meditation in the Daily Life	Vimala Thakar	Shiva-Kuti, Mount Abu
15.	Anatomy of an Illness	Norman Cousins	Bantam Books, New York
16.	Love, medicine and miracles	Bernie Siegal	Arrow books Limited Random House, 20 Vauxhall, Bridge Road, London SW1V 2SA U.K.
17.	Walking	Casey Meyers	Random House Inc., New York
18.	The Art of Loving	Erich Fromm	Unwin Paperbacks, London
19.	Psychoanalysis and religion	Erich Fromm	Bantam Books, New York
20.	Nutritive Value of Indian Foods	C. Gopalan & others	National Institute of Nutrition, Hyderabad
21.	The Seven Habits of Highly Effective People	Stephen Covey	Simon and Schuster
22.	First Things First	Stephen Covey	Simon and Schuster
23.	Meditation for everybody	Louis Proto	Penguin Books

*****

Scientific References

1. Braunwald E. Heart Disease. W.B. Saunders & Co. Philadelphia, USA. 1992.
2. Ockene I. S. and Ockene J. K. Prevention of Coronary Heart Disease. Little, Brown & Co. Boston. 1992.
3. Bryan Willems. Insulin resistance: The shape of things to come, Lancet, 1994; 344:521-24.
4. P, M. Mckeigue, Bela Shah, M.G. Marmot. Relation of central obesity and insulin resistance with high diabetes prevalence and cardiovascular risk in South Asians. The Lancet, 1991, 337; 382-86.
5. Bryan Williams. Westernised Asians and cardiovascular disease: nature of nature? Lancet, 1995; 345; 401-2
6. Prem Pais, J Pogue, et al. Risk factors for acute myocardial infraction in Indians: A case-control study. Lancet, 1996; 348; 358-63.
7. W. Philip T. James, Coronary Heart Disease in Indians, NFI Bulletin, Volume 16, Number 2, p. 1-4, April 1995.
8. C.HD. Fall, D. J. P. Barker, The Fetal Origins of Coronary Heart Disease and Non-Insulin Dependent Diabetes in India. Indian Pediatrics, 1997; 34; 508.
9. C E Stein, C H E Fall, K Kumaran, C Osmaond et al. Fetal growth and coronary heart disease in South India. Lancet, 1996; 348; 1269-73.
10. Deepak Bhatnagar, Inder S Anand, Paul N Durrington et al. Coronary risk factors in people from the Indian subcontinent living in West London and their siblings in India, Lancet, 1995; 345; 405-9.
11. C. Gopalan. Nutrition and Degenerative Diseases in India, NFI Bulletin, Volume 15, Number 1, p. 1-4, January 1994.
12. Stephen Frankel, Peter Elwood, et al. Birthweight, body-mass index in middle age, and incident coronary health disease. Lancet, 1996; 348; 1478-80.

13. Coronary Heart Disease, Supplement to The Lancet, November, 1996; 348 (I): 1-31.
14. Dean Ornish, Shirley E. Brown, Larry W. Scherwitz et al. Can lifestyle changes reverse coronary heart disease? Lancet, 1990; 336; 129-33.
15. Stevens J etal. The effect of age on the association between bodymass index and mortality. N. Engl J Med 1998; 338: 107.
16. Kassirer J P and Anell M. Losing weight – An ill-fated New Year's resolution. N Engl J Med 1998; 338; 52-4.
17. Exercise for health, WHO/FIMS Committee on Physical Activity for Health, Bulletin of the World Health Organisation, 1995. 73 (2): p. 135-136.
18. Friedman M, Rosenman RH. Type A behaviour and your heart. New York: Knopf, 1974.
19. M. G. Marmot, H. Bosma, J Hemingway et al. Contribution of job control and other risk factors to social variations in coronary health disease incidence, Lancet, 1997; 350; 235-39.
20. Dawber TR, Meadors GF, More EF, Jr. Epidemiological approaches to heart disease: The Framingham study. Am J Publ Health 1951; 41: 279-86.
21. Gordon T, Kannel WB. Premature Mortality from coronary heart disease. The Framingham Study, JAMA 1971; 215: 1617-25.
22. Keys A, Aravanis C, Blackburn H, et al. Epidemiological studies related to coronary heart disease. Characteristics of men aged 40-59 in seven countries. Acta Med Scand, 1967; 180; (Suppl 460): 1-392.
23. Worth RM, Kato H, Rhoads GG, et al. Epidemiologic studies of coronary heart disease and stroke in Japanese men living in Japan, Hawaii and California: Mortality. Am J Epidemiology 1975; 102: 476-87.
24. Bruhn JG, Chandler B, Miller MC, et al. Social aspects of coronary heart disease in two adjacent, ethnically different communities. Am J Public Health, 1966; 56: 1493-506.
25. Wolf S, Herrenkohl RC, Lasker J, et al. Roseto Pennsylvania 25 Years later – highlights of a medical and sociological survey. Trans Am Clin Climatol Assoc 1988; 100: 57-67.
26. Berkman LF, Syme SL. Social networks, host resistance, and mortality: a nine-year follow-up study of Alamedia Country residents. Am J Epidemiology 1979; 109: 186-204.

*****